The Science of Common Sense: Best Practical Decision Science Methods

The Science of Common Sense: Best Practical Decision Science Methods

Frank A. Tillman

Deandra T. Cassone

CONTENTS

Acknowledgements

We would like to acknowledge C. L. Hwang for his significant contribution in this field. His books on multiple attribute decision making, multiple objective decision making, and group decision making provide a compilation of decision science methods in these areas and are fundamental in establishing the field of decision science as an area of study.

We would also like to acknowledge our family and friends who continue to support us in our efforts.

About the Authors

Frank A. Tillman, PhD, PE, has a varied career of over thirty years in academia, consulting, and real estate development. He served as department head at Kansas State University for more than twenty years, where he published over fifty professional articles and four books. He has also authored several books for professionals identifying the approaches that work best for solving problems and offering practicable solutions.

Deandra T. Cassone, PhD, PMP, serves as an associate professor in the Industrial and Manufacturing Systems Engineering program at Kansas State University and has been in management at a Fortune 100 company. Her career of over twenty-five years includes consulting, technical, and management roles and has published two books. With an interest in building structured decision making models, she has been awarded numerous business process patents.

Together they have authored *A Professional's Guide to Decision Science and Problem Solving* and *The Science of Common Sense: Best Practical Decision Science Methods.*

Preface

This book contains a selection of decision science methods that have been useful in solving real-world problems. A myriad of methods exist; however, the authors have selected the best practical set of methods they have used to solve a variety of problems. The intent of this book is to provide readers with the best set of methods that are easy to use and easy to explain.

The material is divided into sections that cover multiple criteria and ranking techniques; multiple objectives, which is a trade-off of conflicting objectives; and group decision making. This last area, group decision making, covers both idea generation and expert opinion when data doesn't exist. The authors introduce methods of data analysis and data mining. Also presented is an overview of simulation for problems that are too complicated to use simple methods to solve. In the end, various operating systems can always be modeled with a simulation using such systems as Rockwell's Arena.

Finally, we feel this body of techniques, which have been field tested and proven easy to use and easy to understand, has never been compiled into a single book. This book appeals to the developer of straightforward, practical solutions and should pique the interest of the academic community for further study.

Chapter 1. Background

1.1   Background

We felt there was a need to address the detailed methods that can be used to solve decision making problems. At the same time, we wanted to suggest the steps to structure the problem and use innovative approaches to solve difficult decisions. This book addresses a number of the solution methods, which include simulation, statistics, ranking problems (multiple criteria decision making), solving problems with multiple objectives (multiple objective decision making), and group decision making for consensus building and obtaining expert opinions. We address how to combine available quantitative data and subjective data and how to develop solutions. There are other methods available—such as artificial intelligence, benchmarking, and best practices—that may shed light on data analysis and identifying the best solutions.

In the following chapters of this book, we will explore the methods and show examples of how they are applied. In this book, we will discuss the types of methods and when to use them. These methods are, in our experience, the best methods available to solve problems, and we have used them to solve a variety of problems in different applications. Generally, we combined methods and ended up developing new and innovative approaches to problem solving.

1.2   Real-World Assessment of Methods

Developing robust, analytical solutions, methods, and tools is used to structure problems and provide a sound, analytical basis for the solutions that are generated. The number of tools and methods is vast, and it is very important to recognize and understand each method that should be used in a given situation. Through years of consulting, operating our own companies, and working in a number of corporate situations, we have developed insights into which methods work and which do not in the "real world." This book contains a number of those methods in their analytical form, as well as their practical applications. Our numerous consulting projects and broad experience in industry have led us to this selection of methods that are easy to explain and use.

1.3   Laying the Groundwork

We have a number of guiding principles or fundamental rules when using particular methods to solve problems in corporations and in government.

1.3.1   Rule 1: Select the methods that the decision maker can understand.

Problem solutions must be understood by those who are going to make the decisions. Many corporations have trusted employees who understand analytical methods. However, if they cannot easily explain how the results were achieved to those who must act on the decisions, they will not get the support they need to implement the solutions. We have seen this a number of times in our work and would caution against overcomplicating the solutions, no matter how robust they may be.

One study, which included the allocation of limited resources, was a typical linear programming problem. We developed and used a linear programming model and obtained a number of solutions from a number of "what if" scenarios. We then took each of the solutions to the company's accounting department and had employees there verify the results. We had listed the possible scenarios and had the decision makers pick the one they liked best. We could then tell them that their accounting department employees had verified each one without having to explain how they were determined.

Management did not understand linear programming and how we arrived at the best solutions for each scenario, but they accepted the results because the accounting department verified each solution. Thus it was easy for the decision makers to accept the results. This approach can be used for any complicated analytical method and provides a way for any decision maker to accept the solution.

1.3.2   Rule 2: The decision process must be easy to use.

Decision processes that are complicated, have massive amounts of steps or data to process, or that are not "user friendly" will keep decision makers from using the results. It is better to select a simpler approach that is easy to apply with available data and that can provide solutions quickly.

1.3.3   Rule 3: The model must fit the time frame available for development

When developing a solution to a problem, it is important to understand the expectations by management in regards to the solution development. Individuals in corporations are under pressure to deliver results quickly. A sophisticated model may take months to develop and solve the problem, however, management may look for a result in weeks versus months. An understanding of how to get to an appropriately accurate solution within the time allotted is necessary to meet the demands of the corporation.   An example of this may be an identified need to develop a multiple objective decision making solution, however, timing is such that a simulation model which can be used to search for better results may be all that the time allows. It is important to understand the time frame available for development to provide a solution that is of value to the organization.

1.3.4   Rule 4: The model must be adaptable to an ever-changing corporate environment

Overly complex or rigid models may not be adaptable to the ever-changing corporate environment. New technologies are introduced quickly. Mergers and acquisitions may change the profile of a business. People change and move within a corporate environment so support for development may be limited to the senior executive's tenure in a position. It is important to structure models with the selected environment in mind so that these models can be adapted to these changes quickly.

1.3.5   Rule 5: The model must be linked to achieving the corporate objectives

It is important to have a clear understanding of corporate objectives when developing a model. Without that understanding, solutions generated by the effort may not support the strategic direction of the company.

1.3.6   Rule 6: Lack of data can be supplemented with expert opinion

Sometimes a corporate environment or activities are changing so rapidly that using historical data to forecast future activities will result in an inaccurate forecast. In those cases, expert opinion can be used to supplement or replace historical data in forecasting. Group decision making methods presented in this book can provide a structured approach to capturing this forward-looking forecast information from corporate experts.

1.3.7   Rule 7: Definition of the Optimal Solution

Sometimes when we develop models and solutions, we look for extreme levels of accuracy and improvement within the organization. This may require months of development time and pressure to show ultimate results when the model and solutions are delivered. In our experience, we have redefined an optimal solution to be "Are we doing this better than before in regards to corporate objectives?" Incremental improvements to operations and processes provide value to an organization and their bottom line. Providing the right level of detail and accuracy within a given time frame can show value in the processes and also be a win for structured analytical processes.

The following section discusses solving problems that meet corporate objectives. We feel that this is a fundamental principle to driving activities and solutions that support a company's strategic direction.

1.4   Solving Problems That Meet Corporate Goals and Objectives

Many times, individuals start solving problems without having a clear understanding of the company's goals, their importance, and the data and metrics that are used to measure the performance of a process against corporate goals. We spend a significant amount of time discussing this topic in our previous book, *A Professional's Guide to Decision Science and Problem Solving*, but the key steps in developing goals are shown below.

Step 1:   Establish overall objectives and goals.
Step 2:   Weight the objectives to determine their importance.
Step 3:   Select the decision criteria.
Step 4:   Weight the criteria to determine their importance.
Step 5:   Develop metrics.

It is important that executive decision makers provide clear direction through the company's goals and objectives so decision that are made throughout the organization support those objectives and be measured against them. Group Decision Making techniques, discussed later in this book, can be used to bring the decision makers together to develop clear corporate objectives. The decision criteria and metrics are then developed that can be used to measure and meet those objectives.

We wrote the book *A Professional's Guide to Decision Science and Problem Solving* to establish an innovate method for making critical decisions at the executive level of any organization, either in industry or in government, as well as the factory floor. A new approach is presented that ensures the "best decisions possible." *A Professional's Guide to Decision Science and Problem Solving* lays out clearly a step-by-step method to accomplish this decision process. In this process, the authors address how to define objectives and identify metrics, explore the environment and the problem's scope, and the impacts on decisions. We also evaluate available data and how to extract usable data from standard information systems, i.e., data mining. With the objectives, scope of the problem, and available information, we then select or develop an innovative approach to solving the problem. Benchmarking and best practices are explored. We measure the results by how much we satisfied the goals and objectives of the decision makers. We then do sensitivity analysis and explore the suggested solution for possible changes. See Appendix A for a complete outline of *A Professional's Guide to Decision Science and Problem Solving*.

In this previous book, we assumed the executives had people knowledgeable of the suggested methods. The purpose of this book is to discuss the methods and their application in more detail.

1.5   More than One Method May Be Needed to Solve a Problem

As we discuss methods in this book, we will provide the methods' computational background and real-world examples of where these methods have been used. The examples that are provided demonstrate that in many studies, more than one of the methods discussed are needed to solve a problem. Understanding the data available to solve a problem and data analysis are important in nearly every problem-solving approach, and should support the decision being made. Sometimes data analysis is all that is needed to solve a problem. However, many times data analysis forms a framework for quantifying the problem itself, but serves as an input into other methods that are used to generate solutions. For example, you may use the data that is analyzed to support the decision criteria that is put into a ranking or optimization problem. You also may gather data using the expert opinion process and using group decision making techniques. Examples will be provided in the text, but it is important to realize that many times a combination of methods and approaches is needed to model the operating conditions and develop a robust solution to the problem.

Chapter 2. Overview of Decision Methodologies

2.1   Overview of Decision Methodologies

This chapter provides an introductory survey of tools and methodologies that can be quite valuable in modeling in the decision making environment. At this point in the process, the objectives have been identified, the metrics have been established, and the problem has been structured. The individuals developing the decision model should now look at the types of methodologies available to determine which approach best suits the problem at hand. A basic knowledge of the methodologies presented in this book is useful in order to identify those that have potential use in the model. You can perform a more detailed analysis by selecting a specific methodology that best fits the model of the problem.

Numerous books have been written about each of the types of methodologies listed in the book. The intention here is not to describe these in detail, but to present an overview of some of the best and easily applied techniques that can be used in the decision-modeling process. Methodologies are presented in the following major categories: multiple criteria decision making, multiple objective decision making, group decision making, expert opinion, statistical analysis, forecasting, and simulation.

2.2   Multiple Criteria Decision Making

Decisions that rank alternatives based on several criteria measured with subjective and objective data are best modeled by multiple criteria decision making methodologies. Subjective data is typically forward-looking when compared to objective data, which is historical or looking back. If some objective or historical data are readily available, this can be analyzed with statistics and used, along with the subjective data that is generated with expert systems and used as input to the model. Numerous methods exist and can be applied to multiple criteria decision making models, such as simple additive weights (SAW) or the technique for order preference by similarity to ideal solution (TOPSIS), both of which are discussed later. These two methods are easiest to apply and easiest to understand and provide the best solution.

Examples of multiple criteria decision making models may include the following:

- Selection of executives for promotion or retirement based on performance, evaluation criteria, and need of the organization.

- Ranking critical items for the military based on their contributions to operation plans, readiness, sustainability, and availability.
- Selecting products to keep or delete in a product line based on sales volume, future potential sales, strategic importance, and their impact on operations.

If the time frame for the decision to be made is longer, you can use more sophisticated models to solve the problem. Based on the business conditions, the availability of data, the condition of data, the number of objectives of key decision makers, and the organization's goals, you can combine methods to develop the model.

The following shows a number of multiple criteria decision making methods you can use to develop decision models. See the reference Hwang, et al, for a chart and a discussion of these models. We have identified the easiest to use with available data, and the easiest to understand. These are SAW and TOPSIS for ranking, successive proportional additive numeration (SPAN) for expert group consensus, and brainstorming and brainwriting for idea generation.

2.3   Multiple Objective Decision Making Methods

If the questions to be answered by the model involve the allocation of resources subject to constraints, a single objective or multiple objective optimization model can be applied to the problem, based on the number of objectives identified in group decision making. A trade-off of objectives can be modeled with multiple objective decision making in situations where decisions that are to be optimized involve several conflicting goals and are limited by resource constraints. Numerous methods exist to solve these problems. Examples of multiple objective decision making include the determination of the strategies for the US nuclear arms negotiating team in Geneva, where the objectives are to maximize the United States' total strategic capability and instantaneous strategic capability subject to arms control, force structures constraints. This includes the determination of overall strategies and goals that include long- and short-term goals, such as maximizing profit, while investing in R and D and ensuring an adequate cash flow.

Few of the multiple objective methods, though, allow for a true trade-off of objectives, and the biases associated with these methods must be understood prior to their application as part of the solution methodology. Also, depending on the linearity of the objective functions and constraints, nonlinear programming may need to be applied to an optimization problem to generate the optimal solution. The selection of the optimization model type, a single or multiple objective, and linear or nonlinear method, are dependent on the environment being modeled, the time frame for decisions, and the availability of data to support the model. The ability to generate an optimal solution that is representative of the "real world" is based upon developing a good representation of the problem at hand.

See the chart in Hwang, et al, which shows a number of multiple objective decision making methods (MODM) that can be utilized in developing decision models. The specific method used to combine objectives into one of the standard linear or nonlinear algorithms will be discussed later in the book. For a discussion of these techniques, the reader is referred to C.L. Hwang, etc.

2.4   Group Decision Making

The goal of group decision making is to get a group consensus and determine the objectives that most satisfy the group overall, while balancing the conflicting goals and objectives. These objectives can and do change over time and change when the makeup of the group changes. You can apply numerous methods in group decision making, but the simplest techniques are SPAN, nominal group technique, brainstorming, and brainwriting. Each can be used to gain a group consensus of goals and objectives. You can apply different methods for group decision making based on the expertise, dominance, and political nature of the various decision makers involved in the process. All key decision makers must agree in general about the goals and objectives to be accomplished; otherwise, there is no point in proceeding.

You can also use group decision making when subjective data about the future is the primary data available to support and develop a model. Because it is hard to look into the future, sometimes the one resource to get an estimate of future events is to poll experts in the field. Thus, the methodologies suggested facilitate obtaining a weighted group consensus on future events. This is in comparison to a future forecast of events generated from past statistical data. The basic assumption of statistical models is that the future will behave as it has in the past. In the current business environment, this is seldom true, and no historical data is available. Group decision making is also useful when the problem is complex and difficult to define. The "gut feel" of experts can often provide good information for a model when no other data is available. The time frame for the decision can dictate the type of model and the type of data that can be gathered for use in the model. If the model must be developed quickly, the objectives identified in the group decision making process can be incorporated into a multiple criteria decision making model, discussed later, which can use both objective and subjective data. Typically, multiple criteria decision making models are less complex, thus less time consuming, and are based on ranking alternatives.

2.5   Expert Opinion

Individuals that have been with an organization for long periods of time generally have a great deal of experience about the organization and possess knowledge that can be captured and used for model building. This type of data or opinion is not typically maintained in a database. Many times this data is not easily incorporated into a decision process. Expert opinion can be captured from individuals in a variety of ways. Some examples of how expert opinions can be captured include the following:

- Judgment and opinion about the project's success.
- Opinions about what are the key areas for strategic planning.

- A new product's potential.
- Establishing organizational goals and objectives.
- Ranking available options.
- Rating the decision criteria used to assess projects.
- Providing an assessment of future projections.

Obtaining expert opinions is often overlooked in the decision-modeling process. Expert opinion integrates the knowledge of an individual and how his or her sum total of experience determines his or her perception of the future. With a structured approach, this knowledge can be quantified, captured, and integrated into the decision process.

Much valuable information can be captured from individuals with in-depth knowledge about an organization, and if not obtained this way, it would not be used to help make decisions. An expert opinion is forward looking, while statistical data, on the other hand, is solely based on backward or historical observations. The assumption in statistical models is that the future will be the same as the past, while an expert opinion can capture what will happen in a fast-changing future business climate.

2.6   Statistical Analysis and Forecasting

You can review statistical concepts in detail in various statistics texts and production planning books. Many more sophisticated techniques are available. The purpose of covering the topic in the text is to highlight some readily known basic techniques, which are easily understood and applied, that you can use to gain a great deal of understanding of the data for the model. Statistical functions are readily available in spreadsheets and databases such as MS Excel and MS Access. Techniques that have proven very useful are regression theory, exponential smoothing and moving averages.

2.7   Simulation

Most times, business problems do not fall neatly into one modeling approach. Simulation is a decision making technique that is used to model a real world environment, system, or design and uses that model to analyze the operating characteristics of that environment. Simulation is the process of creating a model of a proposed system and using this model to represent the operating conditions. The model is used to identify and understand those factors that control the system and/or to predict the future behavior of the system. Almost any system that can be quantitatively described can be simulated.

The purpose of simulation is to understand the mechanisms that control the behavior of a system and use that information to make decisions around the feasibility of the design or environment. Once a simulation model has been developed, this model can be used to adapt and test parameters, and then forecast the behavior of a system.

Simulation models can be relatively simple to develop, such as using a Monte Carlo simulation in an Excel spreadsheet or workbook. Or they can be very sophisticated, employing simulation languages and modeling complex system capabilities. The concept of simulation is important in modeling and decision making because it provides a means to represent a real-world (nonlinear) environment, assess how this environment performs, and understand improvements to the environment based on changes to it.

There are several simulation languages, but we find ARENA is very good. The key building blocks in a simulation model include input-output blocks, transfer actions, and results determination. Some languages allow automatic sampling of Monte Carlo or random number generation. The random samples can be taken from a variety of statistical distributions, normal, exponential, beta, uniform, etc. You can input the distribution that best represents your process, and then generate random samples from that distribution. Different distributions can be used within a single model to represent the various phases of the process as various transfer functions. Simulation is used when the process is complicated and cannot be easily analytically defined and modeled.

Chapter 3. Multiple Criteria Decision Making Methods

3.1   Introduction

Decisions that rank alternatives based on several criteria measured with subjective and objective data are best modeled by multiple criteria decision making methodologies. Subjective data are typically forward-looking when compared to objective data, which are historical. If some objective or historical data are readily available, it can be analyzed with statistics and used along with the subjective data that is analyzed with expert systems and used as input to the model. Numerous methods exist and can be applied to multiple criteria decision making models, such as SAW or TOPSIS, which are discussed later. These two methods are easiest to apply and easiest to understand (see Hwang and Yoon).

Examples of multiple criteria decision making models may include the following:

- Selection of executives for promotion or retirement based on performance, evaluation criteria, and need of the organization.
- Ranking critical items for the military under budget constraints based on their contributions to operation plans, readiness, sustainability, and availability.
- Selecting products to keep or delete in a product line based on sales volume, future potential sales, strategic importance, and their impact on operations.

If the time frame for the decision to be made is longer, you can use more sophisticated models to solve the problem. Based on the business conditions, the availability of data, the condition of the data, the number of objectives of key decision makers, and the organization's goals, you can use a number of methods when developing the decision model. Some of the key points considered in using a ranking methodology are discussed below.

3.2   Normalization of Attribute Ratings

Criteria or attribute ratings are normalized to eliminate computational problems caused by a variety and range of measurement units in a decision matrix. It is not always necessary, but it is essential for many compensatory MADM methods. Normalization aims at obtaining comparable scales, which allow inter-attribute as well as intra-attribute comparisons.

Consequently, normalized ratings have dimensionless units, and the larger the rating becomes, the more preference it has.

3.3   Normalized Direct Weighting

This approach is a simple, intuitive weighting approach in which each objective or criteria is given a score and the score is then normalized so the sum of the normalized weights totals to 100 percent. Following is an example of weighting of sample objectives utilizing this approach. Each objective is assigned a score between 1 and 10. From this, a percentage of the total is calculated to represent the normalized weight.

Table 3.1 Normalized Direct Weighting

	Score	Calculation	Normalized Weight
Cost	10	10/50	20%
Risk	7	7/50	14%
Performance	10	10/50	20%
Reliability	8	8/50	16%
Producibility	8	8/50	16%
Maintainability	7	7/50	14%
Total	50		

3.4   Quantification of Qualitative Ratings

An alternative in an MCDM problem is usually described by attributes that are either quantitative or qualitative. How do we compare these two kinds of attributes? We simply set a scale or score for an attribute that is qualitative, thus converting it to a quantitative score.

A set of statements, composed of approximately an equal number of favorable and unfavorable statements covering qualitative attributes, is constructed. For example, the attitude of residents toward the opening of a new plant can be aptly described on a five-point scale as *very unfavorable, unfavorable, neutral, favorable,* and *very favorable.* The Decision Maker (DM) is asked to pick a statement that best describes the given attribute property. To score the scale, the response statements are credited with 1, 2, 3, 4, or 5, reading from unfavorable to favorable. A five-point scale has been applied predominantly in marketing and psychology literature, but a more detailed scale, such as a seven-point or nine-point scale, might be more adequate, depending on the decision-problem context. Since the scale is an interval scale, the intervals between statements are meaningful, but the difference between scale scores have no meaning.

Therefore, a scale system of (3, 5, 7.9, 11) can be utilized instead of (1, 2, 3, 4, 5). Note that the difference between a very favorable and a favorable rating is the same as the difference between a favorable and a neutral rating, which in turn is the same as the difference between a neutral and an unfavorable rating. However, we cannot say that a favorable rating is twice as advantageous as an unfavorable rating, since their ratio on a (1, 2, 3, 4, 5) scale is 2 (= 4/2), and the same ratio on a (3, 5, 7, 9, 11) scale is 1.8 (= 9/5).

The verbal terms used in describing the residents' attitude toward the opening of a new plant may not be appropriate to describe other qualitative attributes. For example, if price is one of the attributes, the possible statements could be {very expensive…fair price, fairly cheap…extremely cheap}. Or, if size is one of the attributes, the possible statements could be {extremely small, very small…medium, medium large…extremely large}. For any type of attribute, we can always find a pair of words that represents extreme meanings, such as high versus low, good versus poor, small versus large, and so on.

3.5   Maximin

The overall performance of an alternative is determined by its weakest or poorest attribute. In such a situation, where a DM does not have prior knowledge about which attribute will determine overall performance (or which link will yield first), the DM should take a pessimistic attitude and choose that alternative whose worst rating is better than the worst rating of the others. If the worst value is acceptable for all alternatives, then we have an acceptable solution. If any of the worst values is unacceptable, we eliminate this alternative. It is the selection of the maximum (across alternatives) of the minimum (across attributes) values, which is called "Maximin" or "best of the worst."

In some instances, we may want a nonlinear difference in scale value, e.g., (1, 3, 7, 12, 20) to emphasize the larger scores. These scores are normalized as before.

The selection procedure has two steps: Determine the poorest attribute value for each alternative, and then select the alternative with the best value on the poorest attribute.

A growing software company needs to select a manager for its newly established East Asia division. The manager will be stationed in Taiwan and will be responsible for the operation of this new division. Six candidates are selected for the position and are evaluated on the basis of five attributes. The data are presented in Table 3.2. Attribute ratings are based on a 10-point scale with a larger-greater preference.

The personnel department therefore uses the Maximin method because they want the best of the possible worst. Since all ratings are on a 10-point scale, comparisons can easily be made directly on attributes where the higher score is the best. First, we find the minimum rating for each candidate (rows), and then choose the maximum among the minimums. The procedure is shown below:

Table 3.2 Criteria Values for Six Managers

Candidates	Attributes					Min	Max	
	X_1	X_2	X_3	X_4	X_5	Min	Max	
A_1	9	5	5	4	7	4	9	
A_2	8	8	9	9	8	(8)	9	← **Maximin**
A_3	10	8	7	8	8	7	(10)	← **Maximax**
A_4	8	5	9	6	5	5	9	
A_5	5	7	5	8	8	5	8	
A_6	8	5	5	6	7	5	8	

Candidate A2 is chosen for the position with the maximum score of 8. Note that his performance does not go below 8 points in any attribute, while other candidates have one or more weak attributes.

3.6   Maximax

In contrast to the Maximin method, the Maximax method selects an alternative by its best attribute rating, rather than its worst. In the Maximax method, only a single attribute represents an alternative, and all other attributes are ignored. The Maximax has two operating procedures: Identify the best attribute value for each alternative, and then select the alternative with the maximum of the best values. For the software company, the Maximax selection is A_3, which is also shown in Table 3.2 above.

3.7   Simple Additive Weighting Method

The simple additive weighting method (SAW) is probably the best-known and widely used method of multiple attribute decision making. To each of the attributes in SAW, the decision maker assigns importance weights, which become the coefficients of the variables. These weighted coefficients need to be normalized. To reflect the decision maker's marginal worth assessments within attributes, the decision maker also makes a numerical scaling of intra-attribute values. The decision maker can then obtain a total score for each alternative simply by multiplying the scale rating for each attribute value by the importance weight assigned to the attribute, and then summing these products over all attributes. After the total scores are computed for each alternative, the alternative with the highest score (the highest weighted average) is the one prescribed to the decision maker.

There are some precautions that are important when developing decision models.

1. Scaling of criteria value can greatly influence the impact of single criteria and thus the ranking. To avoid this problem, all values within a criterion are normalized.
2. Independence: Care should be taken so that all the criteria are independent, thus avoiding overweighing the effects of a single criterion.

Table 3.3 shows an example of evaluating alternatives using the SAW method. Each alternative is evaluated against each of the five attributes or criteria. Two of the criteria, however, have different scaling than the remaining inputs where the scale is from 1 (low) to 5 (high) in the evaluation. The development cost criteria and economic benefit criteria use different scales, which are shown in Tables 3.4 and 3.5, respectively.

Table 3.3 Example of the Simple Additive Weighting Method

| | | Importance Weight | | | | | |
| | | 10% | 25% | 20% | 15% | 30% | |
Alternatives	Development Cost	Development Cost (See Scale)	Inventory Investment (Scale = 1- low to 5- high)	System Interface (Scale = 1-low to 5- high)	Transportation Cost (Scale = 1-low to 5-high)	Economic Benefit (See Scale)	Score
System Enhancements	$ 8,000,000	1	3	5	3	4	3.5
Acquisition Improvements	$ 1,500,000	3	3	3	2	2	2.6
Transportation Optimization	$ 2,000,000	3	2	1	5	4	3.0
Repair Cost Reduction	$ 8,000,000	5	2	1	2	3	2.4

Table 3.4 Development Cost Scale

Development Cost Scale
5 - very low <$500K
4 - low >=$500K to <$1M
3 - medium >=$1M to <$2.5M
2 - high >= $2.5M to <$5M
1 - very high >=$5M

Table 3.5 Economic Benefit Scale

Economic Benefit Scale
1- very low <$500K
2 - low >=$500K to <$1M
3 - medium >=$1M to <$2.5M
4 - high >= $2.5M to <$5M
5 - very high >=$5M

Each of the decision criteria is weighted in this example. Different criteria weights can result in different rankings. The weights are multiplied by the decision criteria values for each of the attributes for an alternative and are summed to represent a score for the alternative. In this case, the alternative, "System Enhancements" will provide the greatest value to the company based on the evaluation of the alternative and the importance weighting of the decision criteria.

3.8 TOPSIS

The technique for order preference by similarity to ideal solution (TOPSIS) is a multiple attribute decision making problem with a number of alternatives evaluated by a number of attributes. The TOPSIS methodology is viewed as a geometric system with m points in the n-dimensional space. TOPSIS is based on the concept that the chosen alternative should have the shortest distance to the best possible attribute assessment values (positive-ideal solution), and have the longest distance from the worst possible assessment values (negative-ideal solution) for each of the alternatives.

An ideal solution is defined as a collection of ideal levels for the attribute levels. An ideal solution, however, is ideal and usually not attainable. The TOPSIS methodology uses concepts to come closest to the best possible answers and furthest from the worst possible answers. The positive-ideal and negative-ideal solutions are used in this methodology to find the best feasible alternative given the options and evaluations available.

Formally, the positive-ideal solution is denoted as
$$A^* = (x^*_1,\ldots, x^*_j,\ldots, x^*_n)$$
where x^*_j is the best value for the jth attribute among all the available alternatives.

The negative ideal solution is denoted as
$$A^- = (x^-_1,\ldots, x^-_j,\ldots, x^-_n)$$
where x^-_j is the worst value for the jth attribute among all the available alternatives.

TOPSIS defines an index called similarity (or relative closeness) to the positive-ideal solution by combining the proximity to the positive-ideal solutions and the remoteness from the negative-ideal solution. Then the method chooses an alternative with the maximum similarity to the positive-ideal solution. TOPSIS assumes that each attribute takes either monotonically increasing or monotonically decreasing utility. That is, the larger the attribute outcome, the greater the preference for benefit attributes and the less preference for cost attributes.

The method presented is a series of successive steps (see Hwang and Yoon, 1987):

Step 1. *Calculate normalized ratings.* The vector normalizations is used for computing r_{ij}, which is given as

$$r_{ij} = \frac{x_{ij}}{\sqrt{\sum_{i=1}^{m} x_{ij}^2}} \quad \text{where } i=1,...,m; \; j=1,...,n$$

Step 2. *Calculate weighted normalized ratings.* The weighted normalized value is calculated as
$$v_{ij} = w_j r_{ij}, \; i = 1,..., m; \; j = 1,..., n$$
where w_j is the weight of the jth attribute.

Step 3. Identify positive-ideal and negative-ideal solutions. The A* and A- are defined in terms of the weighted normalized values:
$$A^* = \{v^*_1,..., v^*_j,..., v^*_n\}$$
$$= \{(\max_i v_{ij} \mid j \in J_1), \{(\min_i v_{ij} \mid j \in J_1) \mid i = 1,..., m\}$$

$$A^- = \{v^-_1,..., v^-_j,..., v^-_n\}$$
$$= \{(\min_i v_{ij} \mid j \in J_1), \{(\max_i v_{ij} \mid j \in J_1) \mid i = 1,..., m\}$$

where
J_1 is a set of benefit attributes, and J_2 is a set of cost attributes.

Step 4. Calculate separation measures. The separation (distance) between alternatives can be measured by the *n*-dimensional Euclidean distance. The separation of each alternative from the positive-ideal solution, A*, is then given by

$$S_i^* = \sqrt{\sum_{j=1}^{n}(v_{ij} - v_j^*)^2} \quad \text{where } i=1,...,m.$$

Similarly, the separation from the negative-ideal solution, A-, is given by

$$S_i^- = \sqrt{\sum_{j=1}^{n}(v_{ij} - v_j^-)^2} \quad \text{where } i=1,...,m.$$

Step 5. Calculate similarities to positive-ideal solution.

$$C_i^* = S_i^- / (S_i^* + S_i^-), \; i= 1,..., m.$$

Note that $0 \leq C^*_i \leq 1$, where $C^*_i = 0$ when $A_i = A^-$, and $C^*_i = 1$ when $A_i = A^*$.

Step 6. Rank preference order. Choose an alternative with the maximum C^*_i or rank alternatives according to C^*_i in descending order.

3.8.1   TOPSIS Sensitivity Analysis

The models and results provide a means to identify the key drivers associated with the assessment of technology development alternatives. You can perform sensitivity analysis on the current ranked list of technology alternatives to determine how much an alternative evaluation criteria must change to move an alternative up or down in the ranked list of projects. The importance weighting of the evaluation criteria and the evaluation scores for the alternatives drive the alternative scoring in terms meeting customer and organizational goals, as shown in the relative closeness generated by the TOPSIS methodology. Sensitivity analysis is useful in identifying the key drivers of the overall value of an alternative. The specific subcriteria evaluations for the alternatives provide the supporting detail to show why certain alternatives received the scores they did and can be used to pinpoint potential areas for improvement and additional trades.

The methodology used to perform sensitivity analysis consists of testing each criteria for each alternative to determine what the value would need to be to move the alternative up or down in rank. To determine the values of the criteria for the alternatives required to move the alternative up in rank, the criteria is incremented one increment closer to the positive-ideal solution. To determine the values of the criteria for the alternatives required to move the alternative down in rank, the criteria is incremented one increment closer to the negative-ideal solution. The ranking (TOPSIS) program is then run and the results are tested against the original ranking to determine if the change in this criteria value has moved the alternative up (or down) in the rank of the alternatives. The incrementing process continues until a value is determined that can move the criteria up (or down) in rank or the incrementing process reaches the positive-ideal (negative-ideal) solution. If the incrementing process reaches the positive-ideal (negative-ideal) solution and the alternative still does not move up (or down) in rank, it is then infeasible to change the specific criteria value to move the alternative up (or down) in rank. This is done for each of the criteria for all alternatives. Also the incrementing process is done on only one criterion value at a time, thus testing each criterion value independent of any other changes made to the other criteria values.

3.9   A Positive-Ideal Solution (PIS) and Negative-Ideal Solution (NIS) for a MADM Problem

Let us consider a product selection problem shown in Table 3.6. The TOPSIS method and the example have been formulated in an Excel workbook and are used for the demonstration of the method. The MADM problem consists of ten alternatives (products) and is evaluated by six attributes (criteria).

Table 3.6 Product Selection Example

Products	BENEFIT Strategic Alignment (1-Low to 5-high)	COST Competitive Barriers (1-Low to 5-high)	BENEFIT Market Growth Potential	BENEFIT Probability of Technical Success	BENEFIT After Tax Margin/ ROI	COST Initial Investment (millions)
Product A	3	1	1%	71%	21%	$ 11.4
Product B	5	3	2%	64%	11%	$ 14.0
Product C	4	2	5%	95%	25%	$ 20.0
Product D	5	4	3%	94%	18%	$ 12.6
Product E	3	3	2%	85%	8%	$ 15.1
Product F	3	2	3%	71%	26%	$ 12.5
Product G	4	3	4%	85%	6%	$ 14.0
Product H	2	2	3%	68%	30%	$ 18.5
Product I	3	3	3%	82%	2%	$ 9.2
Product J	2	4	8%	81%	32%	$ 16.4

The *positive-ideal solution* (PIS) is the solution composed of all the best attribute values attainable. Similarly, the *negative-ideal solution* (NIS) is composed of all the worst attribute values attainable. Table 3.7 shows the PIS and the NIS for this example.

Table 3.7 PIS and NIS for the Example

	Strategic Alignment (1-Low to 5-high)	Competitive Barriers (1-Low to 5-high)	Market Growth Potential	Probability of Technical Success	After Tax Margin/ ROI	Initial Investment (millions)
PIS	5	1	8%	95%	32%	$ 9.2
NIS	2	4	1%	64%	2%	$ 20.0

In general, the PIS (and NIS) in MADM is a hypothetical alternative whose Cartesian product is composed of the most (and worst) preferable values from each attribute given in the decision matrix. Formally, the PIS, A^*, and NIS, A^-, respectively are:

$$A^* = \{v^*_1,\ldots, v^*_j,\ldots, v^*_n\}$$
$$= \{(\max_i v_{ij} \mid j \in J_1), \{(\min_i v_{ij} \mid j \in J_1) \mid i = 1,\ldots, m\}$$

$$A^- = \{v^-_1,\ldots, v^-_j,\ldots, v^-_n\}$$

$$= \{(\min_i v_{ij} \mid j \in J_1), \{(\max_i v_{ij} \mid j \in J_1) \mid i = 1,\ldots, m\}$$

where J_1 is a set of benefit attributes and J_2 is a set of cost attributes.

Preferred solution:

The preferred solution is based on the descending order of the C* for the TOPSIS ranking solution, from largest to smallest.

Step 1. Calculate normalized ratings. Since each attribute is measured on a different scale, an attribute normalization is required.

Step 2. Calculate weighted normalized ratings. The chosen weights for each of the attributes are shown in Table 3.8.

Table 3.8 Attribute Weights

Attribute Name	Strategic Alignment (1-Low to 5-high)	Competitive Barriers (1-Low to 5-high)	Market Growth Potential	Probability of Technical Success	After Tax Margin/ROI	Initial Investment (millions)
Attribute Weights	20%	10%	15%	15%	30%	10%

These weights are multiplied with each column of the normalized rating matrix. The matrix of the combined normalized (Step 1) and weighted normalized (Step 2) matrix is shown in Table 3.9.

Table 3.9 Weighted Normalized Matrix

Attribute Name	Strategic Alignment (1-Low to 5-high)	Competitive Barriers (1-Low to 5-high)	Market Growth Potential	Probability of Technical Success	After Tax Margin/ ROI	Initial Investment (millions)
Attribute Weights	20%	10%	15%	15%	30%	10%
	BENEFIT	COST	BENEFIT	BENEFIT	BENEFIT	COST
Product A	0.0535	0.0111	0.0122	0.0420	0.0970	0.0245
Product B	0.0891	0.0333	0.0243	0.0378	0.0508	0.0301
Product C	0.0713	0.0222	0.0608	0.0562	0.1155	0.0430
Product D	0.0891	0.0444	0.0365	0.0556	0.0832	0.0271
Product E	0.0535	0.0333	0.0243	0.0502	0.0370	0.0325
Product F	0.0535	0.0222	0.0365	0.0420	0.1201	0.0269
Product G	0.0713	0.0333	0.0486	0.0502	0.0277	0.0301
Product H	0.0356	0.0222	0.0365	0.0402	0.1386	0.0398
Product I	0.0535	0.0333	0.0365	0.0485	0.0092	0.0198
Product J	0.0356	0.0444	0.0990	0.0479	0.1479	0.0353

Step 3. Identify positive-ideal and negative-ideal solutions. The attributes in the matrix are both cost and benefit attributes, so the positive-ideal and negative-ideal solution is based on the

nature of the attribute where for a *benefit* attribute, bigger is better, and for a *cost* attribute, smaller is better. The weighted normalized positive-ideal and negative-ideal solutions are shown in Table 3.10.

Table 3.10 Positive and Negative-ideal Solutions

	Strategic Alignment (1-Low to 5-high)	Competitive Barriers (1-Low to 5-high)	Market Growth Potential	Probability of Technical Success	After Tax Margin/ROI	Initial Investment (millions)
PIS	0.0891	0.0111	0.0990	0.0562	0.1479	0.0198
NIS	0.0356	0.0444	0.0122	0.0378	0.0092	0.0430

Step 4. Calculate separation measures. The separation measures from A^* are computed:

$$S_A^* = \sqrt{\sum_{j=1}^{5}(v_{Aj} - v_j^*)^2} \quad.$$

The separation measures from A^- are computed as

$$S_A^- = \sqrt{\sum_{j=1}^{5}(v_{Aj} - v_j^-)^2} \quad.$$

Table 3.11 shows the separation measures for the example.

Table 3.11 Separation Measures

	S*	S⁻
Product A	0.1078	0.0974
Product B	0.1262	0.0709
Product C	0.0590	0.1255
Product D	0.0962	0.0974
Product E	0.1408	0.0403
Product F	0.0795	0.1182
Product G	0.1339	0.0582
Product H	0.0873	0.1336
Product I	0.1579	0.0410
Product J	0.0654	0.1641

Step 5. Calculate similarities to the positive-ideal solution. The value of C_A^* is calculated from $C_A^* = S_A^- / (S_A^* + S^-)$ and is shown as the relative score, which is shown in Table 3.12.

Table 3.12 Relative Score

	S*	S⁻	Relative Score C*
Product A	0.1078	0.0974	0.4749
Product B	0.1262	0.0709	0.3597
Product C	0.0590	0.1255	0.6802
Product D	0.0962	0.0974	0.5030
Product E	0.1408	0.0403	0.2224
Product F	0.0795	0.1182	0.5980
Product G	0.1339	0.0582	0.3030
Product H	0.0873	0.1336	0.6047
Product I	0.1579	0.0410	0.2063
Product J	0.0654	0.1641	0.7150

Step 6. Preference rank order.. Based on the descending order of C_i^*, the preference order is shown below in Table 3.13. In this example, Product J would be the highest-ranking alternative, and if resources are available to fund the investment, it would be selected to pursue.

Table 3.13 Rank Order of Products

Product	Relative Score	Rank
Product J	0.7150	1
Product C	0.6802	2
Product H	0.6047	3
Product F	0.5980	4
Product D	0.5030	5
Product A	0.4749	6
Product B	0.3597	7
Product G	0.3030	8
Product E	0.2224	9
Product I	0.2063	10

Referring back to Table 3.6, we see that Product J has a lower score for strategic alignment (2), lower competitive barriers (4), the highest market growth potential (8 percent), a high probability of technical success (81 percent), and the highest after-tax margin/ROI (32 percent), but it does have a higher initial investment ($16.4 million). The importance weights are drivers in the calculation of the preference score and rank, as well. The authors have used this approach in budget allocation consulting projects where the investment, in this case, the initial investment attribute, is used, along with the rank order, to select projects to fund based on the overall budget for the organization. Using TOPSIS as a backbone for prioritizing projects and allocating resources to projects based on the available resources provides a logical, structured approach to resource allocation.

The importance of sensitivity analysis should be mentioned at this point, as well. We view the initial solution as a starting point in decision making. The weights drive the product ranking and should not be overlooked. We have previously used group decision making techniques to ensure that the weights are representative of the organization. Testing the different rank order of products with different attribute weights can be done as part of sensitivity analysis with the solution. Additionally, testing the modification of the individual attributes can provide decision makers with insight into how sensitive various values are to the resulting rank order. Sensitivity analysis is an important aspect of using structured methods in the decision making process.

3.10   Analytical Hierarchy Process or Eigenvector Method

This approach is based on the decision maker assigning a comparative value of importance for each of the criteria. The criteria are compared against one another, and a relative degree of importance is assigned in the comparison. A rating scale ranging from 1 to 9 is used to assign the degree of importance one criterion has over the other. An example is shown in Table 3.14, where the importance of decision criterion A is more important than decision criterion B, and the degree of that importance is valued at 7 (demonstrated importance).

Table 3.14 Pairwise Comparison of Decision Criteria

Decision Criterion A compared to	Decision Criterion B
1	Equal importance
2	
3	Weak importance
4	
5	Essential or strong importance
6	
7	Demonstrated importance
8	
9	Absolute importance

We note that AHP compares alternatives to one another on a scale that is quite arbitrary. It often leads to the Condorcet problem, where A is better than B, is better than C, is better than A. Those need to be resolved. The number of comparisons can be geometrically increased if you go from five alternatives to ten alternatives. We feel it is better to go deeper and compare the characteristics of each alternative and use individual criteria that each alternative is measured against. We feel AHP doesn't consider the critical information that is available for each alternative, as measured against the characteristics or criteria of each alternative. In contrast, methods such as SAW and TOPSIS do utilize this additional information in making decisions.

The comparison process is stored in a matrix, including the direct comparisons and their reciprocal values, and the normalized Eigenvector value is then computed. This method enables the user to achieve a more finely tuned weighting, but it takes more time to accomplish based on the number of criteria. The more criteria there are, the greater the number of pairs that need to be compared and evaluated. There is a limited number of criteria and alternatives, such as five or six, that should be considered using this method because of the time required for the evaluation and the consistency between the paired comparisons.

The decision maker is supposed to judge the relative importance of two criteria. The number of judgments is $_nC_2 = n(n-1)/2$. There is a method of scaling ratios using the Eigenvector principle of a positive pairwise comparison matrix. This method, while it has software available, is difficult to use for a large number of criteria and is difficult to explain to the decision maker. A comparison has been made between this method and TOPSIS. TOPSIS is much quicker. It is based more on individual criteria values by one or more decision maker and was easier to explain. It also has a sensitivity capability that is difficult to do with the analytical hierarchy process. Thus we recommend the use of TOPSIS or SAW.

Chapter 4. Methods for Multiple Objectives

4.1   Introduction

When a problem or model involves multiple objectives, it falls into the category of multiple objective decision making. This involves one or more objective(s) that may or may not have constraints and may be linear or nonlinear equations.

A trade-off of objectives can be modeled with multiple objective decision making in situations in which decisions are to be optimized that involve several conflicting goals and are limited by resource constraints. Numerous methods exist to solve these problems. Examples of multiple objective decision making include the determination of the strategies for the US nuclear arms negotiating team in Geneva, where the objective is to maximize the US total strategic capability and instantaneous strategic capability subject to arms control, and force structures constraints. Corporations need to include long- and short-term goals, such as maximizing profit, while investing in R&D and ensuring an adequate cash flow in the future.

Few multiple objective methods, though, enable a true trade-off of objectives, and the biases associated with these methods must be understood prior to their application as part of the solution methodology. Also, depending on the linearity of the objective functions and constraints, you may need to apply nonlinear programming. The selection of the optimization model type, a single or multiple objective, linear or nonlinear method, is dependent on the situation modeled and the availability of data to support the model. The ability to generate an optimal solution representative of the "real world" is based upon developing a good representation of the problem at hand. It should be noted that if the process is too complex for multiple objective methods, and the people doing the analysis are under time constraints to get an answer quickly, one should consider a simulation model, which is discussed in chapter 6. Simulation tries a number of scenarios and the one that best fits the objectives is selected.

Demand and other exact or objective quantities can be determined from company data. Some data are subjective and are agreed upon by group consensus of senior management. Most notable is the relative importance of weight of the objectives. The group decision methods can be used to analyze this subjective data. This is covered in the next chapter.

4.2 Multiple Objective Decision Data Requirements

4.2.1 Linear Models

With linear models, the basic model is solved with linear programming software. The two basic approaches are George Dantzig's simplex method, and the sequential numeration algorithm of Karmaker's algorithm. (Software is available for both, e.g., Excel.)

A suggested general approach to solving linear multiple objective decision making (MODM) models is presented below.

4.2.2 Multiple Objective Decision Making (MODM) Method

Multiple objective decision making (MODM) methodologies are used to optimize problems with several conflicting objectives or goals and constraints. The positive and negative ideal solutions are generated, along with the one that corresponds to the maximum achievable goals over all objectives using the available resources. Given these solutions as the starting point, the decision maker adjusts the level of each objective (or goal), noting that to improve one objective, the other objectives are relaxed and decreased. This process is continued until a satisfactory compromise solution is reached. The problem is set up as a linear programming problem with multiple objective functions and the necessary constraints. An initial solution is first calculated that tries to satisfy the goals on variable weights of importance. The user can then reset the goals as he/she sees fit to arrive at a best-compromised tradeoff solution. See Hwang for a taxonomy of a number of available methods.

Formulate the Problem

The MODM model equation formation follows the same basic formation of a linear programming problem with the addition of multiple objectives. Following are examples for formulating the constraints, objectives, and bounds of an MODM model.

1. Constraint example:
   Constraint $2x + 3y \geq 100$
2. Equal ($=$) signs should be included if a $\geq$ or $\leq$ constraint
   Constraint $2x + 3y \geq 100$
3. Multiplication is typically implied.
   Constraint $2x + 3y \geq 100$
4. Objective equations have the same format as constraint equations, except they are preceded by a MIN or MAX to denote whether they are minimized or maximized.
   MAX Objective $2x + 3y$
5. Bounds are typically listed after the objectives and constraints. First the word BOUNDS may separate the constraints and bounds. The bounds are typically listed individually on a

line and refer to a single variable. Also, note we can have unsigned variables, i.e., where variables can be negative or positive.

BOUNDS

$Xx \leq 80$

$Yy \geq 100$

The following is a sample MODM model problem set up with objectives, constraints, and bounds.

MAX Carbo	24 Mlk + 27Bf + 15Brd + 1.1Let + 52OJ
MIN Cholest	10Mlk + 20Bf + 120Egg + 15Brd + 1.1Let + 52OJ
MIN Cost	0.225Mlk + 2.2Bf + 0.8Egg + 0.10Brd + 0.05Let + 0.26OJ
Iron	0.2Mlk +10.1Bf + 13.2Egg + 0.75Brd + 0.15Let + 1.2OJ $\geq$ 12.5
Vitamin A	720MLK + 107Bf + 7080Egg + 134Let + 1000OJ $\geq$ 5000
Calories	344Mlk + 1460Bf + 1040Egg + 75Brd + 17.4Let + 240OJ $\geq$ 2500
Protein	18Mlk + 151Bf + 78Egg + 2.5Brd + 0.2Let + 4OJ $\geq$ 63

BOUNDS

Mlk $\leq$ 6

Bf $\leq$ 1

Egg $\leq$ 0.25

Brd $\leq$ 10

Let $\leq$ 10

OJ $\leq$ 4

Weights of Objectives

The decision maker weights the objectives, which can be entered directly or determined by using some other method, such as the Eigenvector pairwise comparison method. The direct entry of weights allows the user the capability to assign specific values to each of the objectives. The Eigenvector pairwise comparison method gives the user the ability to determine the objective weights based on a subjective comparison of one objective to another. The Eigenvector method is a good weighting approach when the user is uncertain of the assignment of the weights of each objective. See chapter 3 for a discussion of the Eigenvector method.

Compute the Initial Solutions

The MODM model is then solved, first calculating the positive-ideal solution (PIS), the negative-ideal solution (NIS), and then the initial solutions. After the initial solutions have been calculated, a trade-off of the conflicting objectives can then occur. Maximizing or minimizing each of the objectives by itself accomplishes this.

The PIS and NIS are explained later in the example and the solution process below.

An experienced linear program user can also use additional data when running the MODM model to formulate a better solution. This data includes the input data, iterations of the solutions, the final solution, and variables and constraint values with the marginal or shadow prices or dual variables.

Run the Multiple Objective Decision Making Model

Below are the results generated from solving the example.

	MIN Cost	MIN Cholest	MAX Carbo
New Goals	0.00	0.00	0.00
PIS 2.26	8.44	540.00	
MAG	3.15	30.90	441.23
% Achieved	78%	78%	78%
NIS 6.29	110.00	93.34	
Weights	1.00	1.00	1.00

The output contains the positive-ideal and negative-ideal solutions, the maximum attainable goals (MAG) solution by using the weights, the percent achieved for the MAG solution, the current weights, and the new weights could then be entered and the solution process is repeated. The MAG represents the average attained percentage for each objective when they are all solved together. This is done by weighting the objectives, adding them together and setting the sum to an overall Z value. (The formulation is accomplished by setting objective one to z_1, objective 2 to z_2, and so on and then solving them together by adding $z_1 + z_2 + z_3 = Z^*$ and optimizing Z^*.) The user now has the ability to select new goals based on the given information.

Note a minimizing objective can be converted to a maximizing objective by multiplying the minimum objective by negative one (−1).

Notably, goals must fall between the positive- and negative-ideal solutions. The initial solution is a solution that satisfies all of the goals within the given constraints. After the goals are set, the MODM algorithm executes. With every iteration, the MODM program solves a linear programming problem for the primary solution, as well as one for the auxiliary solutions for each of the objectives. The primary solution, in a simple sense, solves the problems with none of the objectives constrained, while the auxiliary solutions solve the problem with a specific objective set equal to the goal. All of the iterations can be reviewed for additional analysis. The information provided from the model includes that which is listed above, as well as the new goal, the primary and auxiliary solutions for the iteration, and the change in the new goal from the previous goal.

New weights for the goals are entered for the objectives. At least one goal must be lower than the primary solution value to make a difference in the iteration for a given problem. The new goals are tested until a satisfactory compromised solution is achieved for the decision maker.

There are several ways to solve a multiple objective problem. One approach is to rank the objectives 1, 2, etc. and solve the problem by optimizing the first objective. Then, add the second objective and optimize it with the remaining resources, ensuring the first objective stays fixed as a solution of the single objective problem. Another way is to weight each objective, add them up into an integrated objective, and solve as a single objective.

A more sophisticated approach is to consider varying weights of each objective until the decision maker is satisfied. This approach is recommended and is illustrated by the above example. MAG is an innovative approach for solving MODM process linear and nonlinear problems.

A more formal process of this method is presented below, in the next section.

4.2.3   Maximum Attainable Goal (MAG) Method

In the above example, we calculated the feasible space for the objectives costs, cholesterol, and carbohydrates. This positive-ideal solution (PIS) is accomplished by determining the best solution by optimizing each objective individually and letting the others be non-constrained. We then calculate the negative-ideal solution (NIS), which minimizes each objective separately to form a payoff table of PIS solutions for each objective and the NIS solution for each objective. See below.

Table 4.1 PIS Payoff Table

	MIN	MIN	MAX
	Cost = f+1	Cholest = f+2	Carb = f+3
f+1	2.26+	2.40	2.51
f+2	9.04	8.44+	10.33
f+3	475.00	490.00	540.00

Table 4.2 NIS Payoff Table

	MAX	MAX	MIN
	Cost = f+1	Cholest = f+2	Carb = f+3
f+1	6.29+	5.88	5.44
f+2	104.00	110.00+	105.00
f+3	96.60	95.40	93.34+

For the MODM problems, the positive-ideal solution is the best or most favorable solution of each objective function, and the negative-ideal solution is the worst or least desirable solution of each objective function. Each objective function value of a preferred solution must be between the best and worst. Since each objective function has a different unit of measurement, i.e., incommensurable units, in general, we need to normalize the objective functions. The PIS and NIS of each objective function are the important elements in the normalization of MODM problems.

The normalized objective functions for the numerical example involve taking the range of values for each objective function by subtracting the NIS value from the PIS and dividing each coefficient value in the objective equation. This ensures that the coefficients are less than or equal to 1.0. After the solution is obtained for each of the objectives' functions, it is divided by its range PIS, – NIS, and the coefficient is subtracted by the NIS, we reverse the process and multiply by $PIS_i – NIS_i$ and divide by the f_i value to get the original objective back.

The preferred solution is the final solution selected by the decision maker. This may or may not be the Maximum achievable goal (MAG), cost = 3.15, cholesterol = 30.90, carbohydrates = 441.23. The percent achieved, 78 percent, is the best amount we can achieve over the range for each objective with the available resources and operating constraints.

The weights are the relative importance of each objective. In this example, it is 1.00 for each objective. Once the MAG is achieved, we then set new goals within the range of PIS and NIS to obtain a new compromised solution; as stated above, we reverse the normalization process to get the actual goals after the solution is obtained. The normalized objective for cholesterol is

$$\frac{10MILK + 20Bf + 120\ egg = 8.44}{91.56}$$

This is shown as

$\dfrac{f_i(x) – NIS_i}{PIS_i – NIS_i}$ for each objective

In the example for each objective, the divisor is

MIN Cost 6.29 – 2.26 = 4.05
MIN Cholesterol 110.0 – 8.44 = 91.56
MAX Carbohydrate 540. – 95.54 = 444.66

The numerator for each objective, we divide by the range into the entire objective equation. Note that for MAX objectives, the denominator and numerator are negative, but cancel out to a positive value.

As stated above, we reverse the normalization process to get the actual goals after the solution is obtained. The normalized objective for cholesterol is

$\dfrac{f_i(x) – NIS_i}{PIS_i – NIS_i} = \dfrac{(10MILK + 20Bf + 120egg – 8.44)}{91.56}$

There are several variations and methods that solve the multiple objectives linear problem with constraints. Some of these are discussed below.

4.2.4   **Goal Programming**

This method has the DM set goals for each objective that is desired. A preferred solution is defined as the one that optimizes the first objective, and an equation is added that sets this objective equal to the solution values. The most common variation of this method also prioritizes the objective (e.g., 1, 2…) in an ordinal way. The goal programming formulates as follows.

The solution for the problem is that h (d^-, d^+) the first objective is minimized first and the solution of this problem is the first objective in an equation. Next h_2 (d^-, d^+) is minimized, but in no case can h_1 be greater than h_1^*. Thus, once the objective h_1^* is achieved, it can never be lowered to the other objective function values. Simply stated, we minimize the first objective and fix it by adding an equation that represents this objective equal to the optimal solution value. This process continues by adding successive equations until the last objective is optimized. This problem is solved using the available linear programming code. Problem examples are shown in Hwang's and Masud's book, *Multiple Objective Decision Making Methods and Applications*.

4.3   Nonlinear Optimization

A number of problems do not fit the usual linear programming problem. There are a number of methods to solve special cases or formulations of nonlinear optimization. In general, these problems are not constrained and deal with the nonlinear objective functions. These popular methods include, Hook Jeeves, sequential unconstrained minimization technique (SUMT), the generalized reduced gradient (GRG), quadratic programming, separable programming, and a whole list of other methods. For a description of these methods we recommend Hwang and Masud's book, *Multiple Objective Decision Making Methods and Applications*. There are a number of other books that treat these problems. There are some limitations in using these methods. First, data usually is so imprecise that fitting the data to the method is so approximate that at best it approximately fits the model. The second is that to study and use these methods requires a knowledge of mathematics usually covered in technical graduate programs such as mathematics, engineering, and statistics.

Since the data generally is so imprecise, we recommend a multiple objective method that is a linear approximation of the nonlinearity. Also, these problems can be solved with linear constraints and standard software.

An example of the approach with two objectives is shown in Figure 4.1. To obtain this figure, set smaller increments or line segments of f_x (x_{ij}) and note the optimal value f^*.

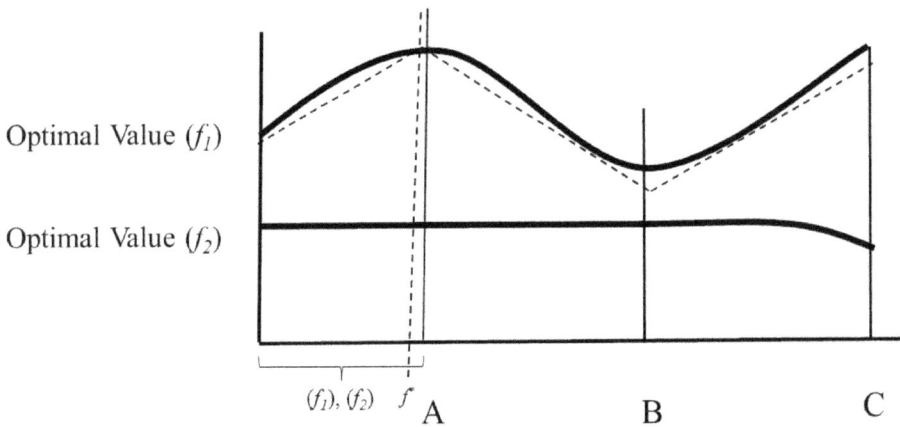

Figure 4.1 Range of the Linear Segments of the Objective and the Optimal Value

The points can then be connected generating the Figure X curves. We then solve three problems, where the solutions are limited by the line segment $O - A$, $A - B$, and $B - C$. We then compare these three solutions for the best combined optimal as our solution. In some cases, one line segment will have a better solution than the other line segments, and not necessarily the same segment. In this case, we weight the w_1f_1 and w_2f_2 and determine which combination has the best overall solutions. This problem is then solved as a multiple objective linear programming problem. We solve problems $f_i(x_j)$ for each set of line segments and pick the best solution.

The variables in $f_i(x_j)$ are incremental by inspecting the shadow prices (dual variables) on the constraints. As the constraints are released for the positive shadow prices, this will improve the $f_i(x_j)$. There is a standard technique, i.e., parametric programming, for doing this. Note the positive shadow prices indicate that the constraints can be changed to improve the objective function fi. All standard linear programming computer codes have this capability of performing parametric programming.

The principle reasons to use these methods are:
1. They allow a wide variety of nonlinear approximations to be solved as linear programming problems.
2. They are fairly nonrestrictive in how nonlinear the problem can be.
3. They permit constraints, and a number of the other nonlinear methods do not.
4. Solutions to the linear multiple objective problems can be solved using a number of standard L.P. computer software codes.
5. Most nonlinear methods do not have computer software available to obtain solutions, and linear programming solutions do.

Again, there is much material on solving nonlinear programming problems where each requires very strict conditions. By converting to constrained multiple objectives linear programming problems, a straightforward solution can be obtained.

Chapter 5. Group Decision Making

5.1   Introduction

Sometimes it is necessary to get the consensus of a group of executives and extract their ideas and expert opinion. We use group decision making to determine the objectives that most satisfy the goals of the organization. These objectives can and do change over time, and they change when the makeup of the group changes. You can apply numerous methods in group decision making, but the simplest and best techniques that we have used are SPAN, nominal group technique, brainstorming, and brainwriting. Each can be used to gain a group consensus of goals and objectives. You can apply different methods for group decision making, based on the expertise, dominance, and political nature of the various decision makers involved in the process. If, however, the group cannot agree in general on the objectives, there is no point in continuing the effort to solve the problem. All key decision makers must agree, in general, on the goals and objectives of the organization that are to be accomplished.

It is also useful to use group decision making when only subjective data is available about the future to support and develop a model. Because it is hard to look into the future, sometimes the one resource to get a forecast of future events is to poll experts in the field, i.e., get expert opinion. Thus the methodologies suggested facilitate obtaining a weighted group consensus on future events. This is in comparison to a future forecast of events generated from past statistical data. The basic assumption of these statistical models is that the future will behave as it has in the past. In the current business climate, this is seldom true, and particularly when no historical data is available. We find group decision making is useful to use when the problem is complex and difficult to define. The "gut feel" of experts can provide good overall information to support a model when no other data is available. The time frame for the decision can dictate the type of model and the type of data that can be gathered for use in the model. If the model must be developed quickly, the objectives identified in the group decision making process can be incorporated into a multiple criteria decision making model discussed earlier, which can use both objective and subjective data. Typically, multiple attribute decision making models are less complex, thus less time-consuming, and are used for ranking alternatives.

There are a number of methods that provide insight into the decision to be made and are presented below. Two methods, Condorcet's Principle and the Borda approach are defined as social choice functions. The remaining techniques in Chapter 5 are classified as either expert opinion and/or group consensus. The method selected is determined by circumstances that involve data availability and/or the operating environment. Sometimes the method that the decision maker feels most comfortable with is selected. It is easier to explain to him and for him to be comfortable with its use.

Now we will discuss Condorcet's Principle and the Borda function.

5.2   Condorcet's Principle

In determining the best rank or preferences, a problem sometimes occurs in which A is preferred to B, which is preferred to C, and where C is preferred to A. This occurs when we directly compare alternatives to one another without using criteria. In the above preference, each alternative is scored against all others.

Condorcet suggests a method to break the cycle and to rank the alternatives. It determines the worst each candidate does against all other alternatives. Then rank each alternative as the best of the worst, so that it is a ranking by the best of the overall worst values.

An example of this is shown in the following table.

Table 5.1 Condorcet's Principle Example

Preference	To			Best of the Worst
	A	B	C	
A	___	15	10	10
B	17	___	12	12
C	21	9	___	9

In the table, A is preferred to B (15) and B (17) is preferred to C (21) and C (21) is preferred to A. When we do the Maximin, we get the rank of B (12) > A (10) > C (9) thus, this is our final rank.

5.3   The Borda Function

The approach that Borda suggests is that we rank each candidate or team 1 through n. Each participant ranks the group of candidates 1 through n and then adds their rank scores (team scores) across each participant. The lowest score is ranked first and so on to the highest score, which is ranked last. This approach is used in the coaches' poll of football rankings, where each coach ranks all teams 1 through n and then adds across each team and the one with the lowest score is ranked first.

5.4   Expert Opinion/Group Participation

The approaches described in the following discussions have been classified by their purpose of generating information and ideas. We then poll the experts and participants for their evaluation, classification, and selection.

5.5   Brainstorming

Brainstorming is a widely used method for idea generation. It is most effective when a set of rules is understood and followed. The first rule is to defer judgment, so ideas are generated freely and the participants feed on one another's ideas and generate a larger number of possibilities. This is done to delay judgment, which stymies new thoughts. Judgments can be made later. Another reason is that the more ideas produced, the better the ideas; thus, with more ideas generated, there is a higher probability of finding the best solution. The judgment of ideas and the solution is completed after most ideas are generated. If it is done too soon, it stymies the flow of ideas.

The rules for conducting brainstorming sessions is to write down the ideas generated in a freewheeling session.

The rules are simple.

1. Do not criticize ideas until the generating phase is done. Evaluation and combination of ideas are done during a later phase.
2. The more the session is freewheeling, the more it encourages participants to suggest any idea they think of when seeing other ideas. The ideas should not be immediately evaluated, so new ideas aren't stymied.
3. The greater the number of ideas, the higher the probability that a good solution can be found.
4. Continued combination of and improvement of ideas opens up many more good solutions. What can occur is that two or more ideas are combined, which generates better solutions or other ideas. They can be tweaked later and extended to get an even a better solution.

The leader needs to keep reminding the group of the problem at hand and keep the group somewhat focused. He/she should go over the rules, ensuring ideas are written down and are evaluated after the generation phase is completed. This does not mean that new ideas should not be permitted as the evaluation progresses. A good size group is made up of six to twelve participants. The well-defined problem is presented to the group by writing it down on flipcharts. The ideas are also written down on the flipchart for all to see. The above rules should be presented and discussed. About sixty minutes is a good length for a session. The advantage of this approach is that it produces a large number of ideas in a short period of time. One disadvantage is that it is sometimes difficult to control the focus of the group. The more structured the process, the better, but they keep generating ideas.

5.6   Brainwriting

The process of brainwriting is similar to brainstorming, but ideas are written down rather than communicating them orally with the leader. All ideas are written down on a sheet of paper and put on the center of the table. Then the leader takes the paper with the ideas written on it and it is passed around and added to by each participant. After a period of time, say thirty minutes, the sheets are gathered for later evaluation. Using this procedure, all participants can share their ideas on an equal basis. A dominant personality will not take over the process and push only their ideas. Reading others' ideas on paper, the process is continued until the improvement of ideas stops. The process is not suitable for large groups. Again, the rules of the process are reviewed with the participants and they are the same as in brainstorming.

This is a simple process and it forces all members of the group to participate. This then ensures a number of ideas are generated and will provide a good solution. A number of variations are possible subject to the approval of the group as members, e.g., the number of ideas and varying time limits.

5.7   The Nominal Group Technique (NGT)

Nominal group technique (NGT) combines elements of brainwriting, brainstorming, and voting techniques. It creates a robust method that is widely used for idea-generation and problem-solving and for a wide variety of applications. The name "nominal" comes from considering a collection of individuals as a group "in name only" or "nominal," since there is no verbal exchange permitted. Generating ideas nominally in a group minimizes confirming influences. It ensures all participants can contribute equally in the group decision.

We will go through the process assuming we are conducting a meeting where we identify the problem, generate ideas for the solution, explore the possible options, and set priorities.

Step 1: Group meeting; the group has five to ten members who have experience, expertise, or knowledge of the problem. Discussion is an exploratory investigation into the problem, defining the scope and use of the solution, and the detail required to develop a usable solution.

Step 2: The group writes down their ideas on a form without discussing them with any other participants.

Step 3: The ideas are recorded after a period of time, e.g., ten to fifteen minutes, on a flipchart that the group can see. Then participants go around the table and ask for one idea from each of them and keep repeating that process until a good number of ideas have been presented.

Step 4: At this step the group needs to clarify, discuss, and defend various ideas or add new ideas. This step allows the group to agree or disagree with the ideas without argument.

Step 5: Aggregate the judgment of the members of the group by writing down on cards their best seven ideas. The best idea is numbered 1 and the worst is numbered 7. Then do a Borda addition, i.e., add the score of each idea across all participants to get an aggregate score. Tally the results, listing the best to worst on the flipchart so all can see.

Step 6: Discuss the results and ranking of ideas and change any the group wants to change. This step is not intended to have an individual change his or her original vote. It is just a review and checking results to get a final listing and ranking of ideas.

This method has the same benefits as brainwriting and eliminates strong personalities that may influence the decision. It also avoids jumping to conclusions too quickly and ensures a thorough analysis of ideas before the final list and priority are selected.

5.8   Surveys

Surveys for problem solving are used to quickly gather data that is not normally available and to get a better understanding of the environment. This is particularly true using the Internet and e-mail. It also provides insight into the process details.

Surveys are conducted via face-to-face meetings, over the Internet, by telephone interviews, and mailed questionnaires. Generally there are several steps involved in conducting surveys.

1. When designing the survey form or questions, make sure you're gathering the information that is needed to solve the problem. Try to ensure the information has maximum accuracy and is used to answer questions from experts. Ensure that the survey is not too long and can be answered quickly. Do not collect extraneous information or data. Be sure the answers can be summarized and recorded easily.
2. Determine the sample size and who is to be surveyed. Survey mostly those people directly involved with the problem and some others familiar with it to get their perspective.
3. Get the results of the survey and group the results to answer the questions that relate to the objectives of the survey. Review the survey results and record the results so they can be analyzed, usually with a numerical scale—that is, as a number or as a percentage of a total.

Surveys are used to document what is currently going on in the process and possibly the percent of time on an activity. Also, it can indicate how frequently various tasks are done compared with the total activities. It can show which people, along with their skill mixes, are required to do the task. This approach is very helpful for manpower planning. It is also useful in getting unavailable data quickly for problem analysis. Using the Internet for your survey forms is a good way to quickly get the results and classify and analyze these results. Since the process is quick and data is so easily gathered, surveys should be used more frequently to track the progress of process improvement efforts.

5.9   Benchmarking and Best Practices

Benchmarking and the use of key performance indicators, a balanced scorecard, or a dashboard are all similar. All of these areas identify and quantify different performance characteristics of a company, typically within an industry. Benchmarking's primary focus is to compare internal performance with external benchmarked performance. Key performance indicators (KPIs) are the metrics deemed essential to understanding the operational health of a company. Measuring performance allows an organization to objectively determine what is working and what is not. The metrics or KPIs established for a benchmarking effort are compared to those of other companies to determine areas of potential improvement and to identify best business practices in an industry.

Numerous companies provide intra-industry and cross-industry benchmark metrics. Developing and using benchmarks provides a concrete measure of your company's performance against others' performances. Books, industry organizations, companies performing benchmarking services, government data, and many other sources of information can be used to develop the hierarchy of criteria.

Those involved with benchmarking must avoid having a "one-size-fits-all" approach, which may not identify specific operating philosophies within a company. Not all types of "best practices" are "best practices" for all companies. You must be careful, though, to analyze the best practices of others in light of their culture and circumstances, or you may find that your efforts do more harm than good. Metrics should be tailored to capture data that is readily available across an industry.

Some sources for benchmarking are easily found, while others may be difficult because some companies are not willing to share that information. Benchmarking data are available to the public or can cost tens of thousands of dollars to access. Here are some potential sources for benchmarked data:

1. Industry trade associations
2. Malcolm Baldridge and other quality awards, where the recipient is obliged to share practices
3. American Productivity and Quality Center of Excellence
4. Informal networks of companies that practice benchmarking
5. Companies providing services for benchmarking in various industries. Examples include PricewaterhouseCoopers, Industry Weekly, Performance Measurement Group, the Benchmarking Network, Manufacturing Performance Institute, Best Manufacturing Practices of the Department of Defense, and many others.
6. Look at the SEC filings of your competitors or companies that are similar industries and have similar processes.

Benchmarking identifies competitors that are doing better than your company. The goal then is to identify how other companies are achieving these better results. This leads to investigating best practices across industries to identify areas to improve operations and resulting performance. Benchmarking goes beyond the metrics and extends to the analysis, adoption, and development of best practices within your own company.

5.10   Delphi Method

The Delphi Method is a combination of brainwriting and survey methods. The object of this method is getting a reliable consensus of a group of experts. It attempts to do this through a series of detailed questionnaires along with expert opinion feedback.

There are two main groups required for this approach: the decision makers and the respondent group of experts.

The Delphi method has several components: anonymous participation, controlled iterations, feedback, and statistical results. The number of iterations of the questioner is normally three to five. Additional iterations depend upon the degree of agreement and the direction of the respondents from their feedback information.

Generally, the first questionnaire asks the experts to respond to a broad question. Information is gathered from the first response and a second and subsequent questionnaire are developed from the previous responses. The goal is to develop several specific answers to address and solve the overall problem. Each successive questionnaire refines the prior questionnaire because it focuses on the best approach. Each stage should include a vote or preference on each previous solution and identify any subquestions on improving the suggested solution.

The format of the questionnaire should make it easy for the expert respondents to develop the final list of approaches or estimates and a priority for each of them. The final report should contain a summary of results and their preference. The Delphi Method provides the input of experts through surveys without having to physically get together.

This approach ensures that no one dominates the process and preserves the ability to change one's mind, as sometimes happens in a public environment. A wide variety of experts who are geographically spread out can participate easily.

The main difference between Delphi and NGT is that Delphi participants do not meet, while NGT participants do meet one another. The following is an example of the Delphi process.

The general problem is to determine the best way to manage inventory and distribute products. The first round of questionnaires would have two broad choices:
1. Have an outside contractor manage both inventory and distribution.
2. Manage inventory inside and distribute both internally and with an outside contractor.

These questionnaires contain these two options. The questionnaires are gathered and stated as follows for the second round.
1. Outside contractor manages the inventory and distribution.
2. By doing this option, with say FedEx, they have an excellent tracking system that can provide better inventory control, and they have a worldwide distribution network.
3. Manage the inventory inside, which enables the restocking to be done quickly, also returns can be restocked and quickly repaired. The distribution would be done by a company fleet and also with the use of contractors.

The third questionnaire is submitted after some detailed time and cost estimates are provided.

1. The inventory is kept outside in a FedEx warehouse and shows movement statistics. Reordering is done daily.
- The cost per unit for this inventory management system is

Inventory = $2.50/unit.

The distribution costs per unit on average is

Distribution = $3.51/unit.

The sum of these two costs is $6.01, with the added benefit of instant tracking and fast delivery, which requires less inventory safety stock investment. The savings is estimated to be $1.22/unit delivered for a total cost of

Total cost (outside) = inventory $2.50 + distribution $3.51, less inventory investment for a savings of $1.22. Thus, total cost = $4.79

2.   Manage the inventory in-house. This requires warehouse space and utility costs, which are estimated to be $1.75/unit.

•   The distribution costs include fleet costs and subcontractor costs of an average $4.39/unit. The total cost for in-house inventory management and distribution are

Total cost (inside) = inventory management cost $1.75 + distribution cost $4.39 = $6.14

After this round, everyone agreed that the cost of outside management had a savings of $6.14 – $4.79 = $1.35/unit.

Thus the Delphi Method was used to clarify the options and generated details to consider in subsequent rounds to obtain the best solution.

5.11   Successive Proportional Additive Numeration (SPAN)

The successive proportional additive numeration (SPAN) has been used in many modern decision making applications in various domains with a good level of success.

SPAN is a voting process that polls experts' judgments. This group consensus technique allows individuals of a committee to have different weights of importance on issues. The individuals are assigned a number of votes (usually an equal number), which are allocated between the options and the experts. Then, each of the experts assigns a percentage of the votes to each of the other experts and to each one of the options.

Basically, if the members of the group feel some of the other experts are more knowledgeable, some of their votes are assigned to these experts.

Using the original distribution percentage selected by each individual, the process continues through successive allocation cycles until all of the original points have been distributed among the options.

The detailed steps for the SPAN method are as follows:

1. Each individual is allocated a quota of points starting the process, usually 100 points.

2. Individuals distribute all these points among options and other members. It is generally recommended that at least a small percentage be allocated to one or more of the options.

3. Each individual allocates a specific percentage of votes to each option and to each of the experts. The actual number of points allocated to each option depends upon overall percent allocation to the options. The proportion is fixed in the subsequent cycles.

4. The process calculates the actual allocation for each option and experts based on the allocations in steps 2 and 3. Using a manual approach or computer program, the process continues through as many successive cycles as needed to distribute all of the points among the options. The process ends when the cumulative total points left with each expert is very close to or equal to zero (<0.1%).

5. The option with the highest number of points is selected as the consensus of the experts.

This process has been shown to be intuitive in various voting methods. In its traditional form, numerical proportional percentage votes are made regarding the allocation of points to experts and options.

The advantage of the SPAN method is it provides a method for generating subjective data by a group of experts.

5.12   Example of SPAN

Three members need to select one option from a set of two options. Each individual is given a packet of 100 points. Then, the individuals establish the percentages they wish to use in allocating points to members and the options. Table 5.2 shows that member A allocates 70 percent of his votes to the options and 30 percent to other members. Among the options, option 1 receives 76 percent of the available votes, and option 2 receives 24 percent. Also, member A directed 100 percent of the allocated votes to member B. Since he assigned 30 percent to members, this parcel has 30 points. At this point, option 1 is assigned 53.2 points (76 percent of 70 votes), and option 2 gets 16.8 points (from member A).

Table 5.2 Percentage Allocation of Points Received at Successive Iterations

Target	Member A	Member B	Member C
Members (A, B, C)	30	60	80
Options (1 and 2)	70	40	20
Member A	0	95	0
Member B	100	0	100
Member C	0	5	0
Option 1	76	25	0
Option 2	24	75	100

The process continues until all the points are allocated to options, as shown in Table 5.3. The outcome of the process is that option 1 gets 158.4 points, and Option 2 gets 141.6 points (out of the possible 300 points). Thus, option 1 is selected as a better alternative.

Table 5.3 Votes Allocation during the First Eleven Cycles

Cycle or Iteration	Final Parcel		Cumulative Votes		Votes Remaining
	Option 1	Option 2	Option 1	Option 2	300.00
1	63.20	66.80	63.20	66.80	170.00
2	41.32	43.18	104.52	109.98	85.50
3	35.31	17.04	139.83	127.02	33.15
4	8.06	8.42	147.89	135.44	16.67
5	6.89	3.32	154.77	138.76	6.47
6	1.57	1.64	156.35	140.40	3.25
7	1.34	0.65	157.69	141.05	1.26
8	0.31	0.32	157.99	141.37	0.63
9	0.26	0.13	158.26	141.50	0.25
10	0.06	0.06	158.32	141.56	0.12
11	0.05	0.03	158.37	141.59	0.05

We have covered the most common decision making methods that are the easiest to use and to explain. They are multiple attribute decision making, discussed in chapter 3, multiple objective decision making, discussed in chapter 4, and group decision making, discussed in chapter 5.

In the next chapter, we will discuss simulation.

Chapter 6. Simulation

6.1   Introduction

Most multiple objective models are measured in discrete time units. Simulation models, however, model transactions over a period of time. Typically, in simulation models, rules of thumb, ranges of values, and Boolean decisions can be included or imbedded via expert systems to develop a realistic representation of a real-world environment. Applying simulation and expert system techniques enable one to model complex situations without connectivity. Simulation enables decision makers to approximate an environment and explore parameters to develop a "better solution." While simulation does not guarantee an optimal solution, a better solution can be achieved with a realistic simulation model of the environment by exploring a number of scenarios varying business constraints, operating rules, and costs.

6.2   Simulation

Simulation is the process of developing a representation of a system in the form of a model so that the system can be tested and studied to determine its performance and behavior. Simulation is used before an existing system is altered or a new system is built to determine its ability to meet specifications, identify issues or bottlenecks, and reduce operating risk. Simulation can be a discrete event simulation, where the system changes instantaneously in response to certain discrete events. Continuous simulators attempt to quantify the changes in a system continuously over time in response to controls. Discrete event simulation is less detailed than continuous simulation, but it is much simpler to implement and can be used in a variety of situations.

6.3   General Steps in Developing a Simulation Model

The steps involved in developing, designing, and analyzing a simulation model are as follows.

Step 1. Identify the problem.
This step involves identifying and documenting the problem you are looking to solve with the simulation model. The problem may be identified from an existing operational issue in a

corporate, military, or public sector environment. Additionally, simulation is a very beneficial tool for testing and modeling new products and services to gain insights into their operational performance.

Step 2.   Formulate the problem.

This step involves having a comprehensive view of the problem that you are looking to solve. A number of key factors should be taken into account in the formulation of the problem:

- Goals and objectives of the study
- Goals and objectives of the system being evaluated
- Performance criteria to be tested
- Operating components of the system being modeled
- End user requirements of the system
- Bounds of the system being tested

Step 3. Collect data to represent the system.

This involves collecting the data that will be necessary to model the system with the simulation. The data used in the simulation may need to be statistically analyzed so that the appropriate type of distribution can be input into the simulation language. If objective data is not available, subjective data or expert opinions may be used to fill in the gaps. Additionally, you may need to develop system or process models to represent the system architecture, interactions, and interfaces of the components of the system.

Step 4. Develop the simulation model.

This step involves utilizing the analysis and statistics and the operating architecture of the system to represent the model in an analytical framework. Normally, a simulation language is used, such as ARENA. It has a number of applications that can be used as guides. This is discussed later in this chapter.

Step 5. Design the simulation experimental runs.

In this step, you determine the conditions around the simulation. In the previous step, you developed the operating framework of the model. Here you will want to determine the parameters and results you will be testing in the simulation. There may be certain bottlenecks that you are looking to evaluate, so parameters associated with the function can be set and tested so you can see the impact of increases or decreases in capacity. A documented plan of the parameters and output to test and their associated results will assist in this process. This also can be an iterative process, where the results from the simulation runs may lead you to test new conditions and parameters.

Step 6. Run the simulation.

Based on the plan and design of the experimental runs, the actual simulation is conducted. Computer applications that support simulation models have a number of capabilities to support running the simulation.

Step 7. Analyze the results.

The results of the simulation runs are gathered and analyzed. The results of the analysis may dictate changes to the simulation model itself, such as additional experimental design changes and modification of the model, so it becomes more representative. The objectives of the simulation are compared to the results to determine whether the information gathered from the model is meaningful to the analysis at hand.

Step 8. Document the simulation model.

The simulation model, the experimental runs, the analysis of the model, and the conclusions drawn from the simulation are documented in this step. Documentation is important to enable the analyst to communicate the assumptions, parameters, results, and the conclusions so decisions may be made on the implications of the study and changes that may need to be made to improve performance.

Many of these steps will be iterative and adjustments will be made to the model as the analysis process is conducted. However, these form the primary activities required in the model development.

6.2   Monte Carlo Simulation Basics

A Monte Carlo method is a technique that involves using random numbers and probability to solve problems. S. Ulam and Nicholas Metropolis coined the term Monte Carlo Method in reference to games of chance (Metropolis and Ulam, 1949).

Computer simulation has to do with using computer models to imitate real life or make predictions. When you create a model with a spreadsheet like Excel, you have a certain number of input parameters and a few equations that use those inputs to give you a set of outputs (or response variables). This type of model is usually deterministic, meaning that you get the same results no matter how many times you recalculate.

Monte Carlo simulation is a method for iteratively evaluating a deterministic model using sets of random numbers as inputs. This method is often used when the model is complex, nonlinear, or involves more than just a couple of uncertain parameters. A simulation can typically involve more than 10,000 evaluations of the model, a task that in the past was only practical using super computers. By using random inputs, you are essentially turning the deterministic model into a stochastic model.

The Monte Carlo method is just one of many methods for analyzing uncertainty propagation, where the goal is to determine how random variation, lack of knowledge, or error affects the sensitivity, performance, or reliability of the system that is being modeled. Monte Carlo simulation is categorized as a sampling method because the inputs are randomly generated from probability distributions to simulate the process of sampling from an actual population. Because of this, we choose a distribution for the inputs that most closely matches data we already have, or best represents our current state of knowledge. The data generated from the simulation can be represented as probability distributions (or histograms) or converted to error bars, reliability predictions, tolerance zones, and confidence intervals.

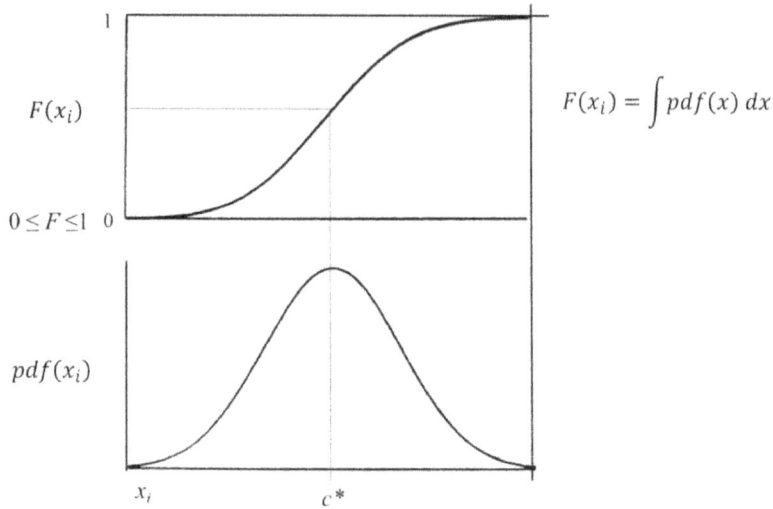

Figure 6.1 Distribution Formulation for Monte Carlo Simulation

The steps in the Monte Carlo simulation that correspond to the uncertainty propagation are shown below, and they can be implemented in Excel for simple models.

Step 1: Create a parametric model:

$$F(x_i) = \int pdf(x) \, dx$$

Step 2: Generate a set of random inputs, $0 \leq F \leq 1$.
Step 3: Determine the x value C* from the probability distribution function (*pdf*) graph shown in Figure 6.1.
Step 4: Repeat steps 2 and 3 for $i = 1$ to n.
Step 5: Analyze the results using histograms, summary statistics, confidence intervals, etc., and select the solution that maximizes the objective.

Since $F(x)$ ranges from $0 \leq F \leq 1$, we use a random number generator between 0 and 1. The cumulative distribution $F(x)$ has a uniform distribution where $F(x)$, $0 \leq F(x) \leq 1$. We get a random number and trace it to the curve on the $F(x)$ curve and drop down to the corresponding points on the probability distribution function (*pdf*) function and get our x value. See Figure 6.1. The process can be used for any *pdf* for any distribution. The process can be used for discrete and continuous distributions.

6.3 Commonly Used Simulation Program—ARENA

Rockwell Automation, Inc. owns a commonly used simulation program, ARENA. It uses the SIMAN processor and simulation.

Simulation software today can be used to model just about any process someone could face. Some examples are the start and stop of an assembly line due to a product change, machine failure rates, conveyors, both guided and unguided vehicles used to transport material from one station to another using individual or palleted items, defective products, the flow of people through a system such as a hospital emergency room, and essentially any other possible situation in which a logical process can modeled to create a simulation of a given event.

These simulations can be built around events that simply occur at a given time, such as a morning delivery of parts, as well as using many different statistical distributions. The software also possesses the ability to help fit collected data to the most accurate statistical curve. This helps to create a more realistic simulation, allowing for variances in the process itself, machine breakdown events and repair times, as well as trucks arriving to pick up finished goods.

The use of a limited queue also simulates events in which there may be space or lines, such as a person arriving at a bank, but seeing four people ahead of her, so she either stays or leaves based on a statistical distribution.

With the advances in processing power, very complex simulation models can now be run thousands of times within minutes or hours to give you a greater sample size. Furthermore, there is a seeding process that creates variants to make up for the computer's inability to truly be random. There are also visual capabilities now that can show a lifelike setting where the simulation is taking place.

There are tutorials for ARENA to show step-by-step processes with ARENA Visual Designer. These applications have icons that can be "dragged and dropped" to build models. To see these tutorials for ARENA you can simply search the Internet for "Rockwell Software—ARENA Visual Designer," and see the applications and tutorials available for review.

In chapter 8, we present a brewery example. It discusses a complex model with stages that must be completed:

1. Data analysis to determine product demand.
2. Use of a linear programming model to allocate resources to products where products have been prioritized with TOPSIS.
3. A general overview and list of products to be made at each brewery on a weekly time frame.

With this information used as inputs for a simulation model that represents a shift or eight hours, random demand data was input into the simulation model, and each solution was generated for various times in the year. These solutions were combined into a probability distribution. From this data we could determine how much inventory space was needed for various times of the year and with seasonal adjustments.

Chapter 7. Data Analysis and Methods

7.1   Introduction

You can review the process statistics presented in this chapter in detail in various statistics texts and production planning books. The purpose of listing the topics here is to highlight some readily known basic techniques that are easily understood and applied. Statistically analyzing available data allows one to gain a great deal of understanding of the data for the model. We are not presenting a study of statistics, but simply pointing out concepts useful in data analyses.

7.2   Standard Statistics

Here are some standard statistics you can use to analyze current and historical data. These statistical functions are readily available in Microsoft Excel or Microsoft Access software programs.

- **Mean:** the arithmetic mean or average of the data set.
- **Low:** the lowest value in the data set
- **High:** the highest value in the data set
- **Median:** the value that represents the middle of the data set when ordered, if there are not equal occurrences above and below the median, an average of the two middle values is taken
- **Mode:** the most frequent value in the set of data
- **Standard deviation:** the measure of dispersion of a frequency distribution; it is the square root of the arithmetic mean of the squares of the deviation of each class of frequencies from the arithmetic mean of the frequency distribution
- **Variance:** the measure of dispersion of a frequency distribution; it is the arithmetic mean of the squares of the deviation of each of the class frequencies from the arithmetic mean of the frequency distribution

7.3   Histogram

A histogram is a representation of a frequency distribution divided by classes of data and plotted according to the frequency of the occurrence for each of the classes of data against another axis, for example, time, failures, and so on. A histogram can be developed using a line graph or with bar graphs, whichever is the typical representation for the environment. Most likely, the data used to develop the histogram will be represented by integer groupings, that is, 1 day or 2 days, or the data can be grouped into ranges such as 0–3 days, 4–6 days, and so on.

7.4   Frequency Distribution for the Data Set by Deciles

This is similar to the development of the histogram; however, the frequency distribution would be divided into classes (e.g., ten classes) of data such that each class contains the same number of individual data points. Ranges or averages associated with each of the classes of data would be displayed on a graphical plot of the information and it can also be displayed in tabular form.

7.5   Determining Safety Stock and Production Variability

If the modeling environment requires the determination of safety stock to cover the variability in a process, statistical analysis is useful for this purpose. The ability for a company to have product on hand, to know how much, or to make an informed decision not to have product on hand, directly impacts the end-user level of satisfaction of the company's service. Costs, production, and capacity considerations may impact an organization's ability to meet safety stock requirements. However, the ability or inability to supply product to customers directly impacts the bottom line of a company's operations in a number of ways. Using statistical analysis gives you insight on this variability, and helps you to determine how to minimize its impact. Wide variability indicates the process is out of control and should be studied to reduce it.

You can translate this statistical analysis of the variability of the process into safety stock levels maintained so that a supplier has a predetermined amount of product on hand regardless of the demand and production variability. For example, you can set safety stock levels so that a product is on hand 95 percent of the time, based on the statistical analysis of the variability of the process. This would mean that you would run out of a given product only five times out of one hundred, or 5 percent of the time, based on the average sales and the average amount of product maintained in inventory. Often, different products have different safety stock requirements. Management may state that its flagship products should never be out of stock. You would set the safety stock levels for these products high in this case. However, when setting safety stock levels, you must also consider the amount of storage space required, the cost of the product to be in inventory, as well as the variability in production and sales.

7.6   Forecasting

A number of forecasting methods are discussed below. You can use a number of different forecasting techniques to predict future occurrences based on historical data. The most common of the techniques are moving averages, exponential smoothing, and multiple regression analysis. These techniques are discussed in much more detail in a number of statistics books.

7.6.1   Moving Averages

A moving average is a forecast of a future occurrence of an activity based on the most recent occurrences of the activity. The simple moving average is the arithmetic mean of the n most recent observations. Here are several characteristics of this model. First, equal weights are assigned to the most recent n observations. Second, each new estimate is computed by adding the new data point and discarding the oldest data point for the previous nth period. Thus, each new estimate is an updated version of the preceding estimate. Third, the rate of response of the moving average to changes in the underlying data pattern depends upon the number of periods included in the moving average. In general, the more periods included in the computation, the less sensitive it will be to changes in the pattern of the data. Conversely, a small value of n leads to a moving average that responds relatively rapidly to changes and may have much more variability. (See section 7.7, below.)

7.6.2   Weighted Moving Averages

A weighted moving average forecast is based on utilizing the concepts of a moving average; however, the most recent observations may possibly be weighted more in the forecasting process. The weighted moving average enables the observations to be weighted such that more importance can be attached to the more recent observations. The weights should be normalized and sum to one. (See section 7.7.1, below.)

7.6.3   Exponential Smoothing

In the exponential smoothing method, new forecasts are derived by adjusting forecasts made for previous periods by considering their forecast errors. In this way, the forecaster can continually revise the forecast based on past experience. This model has the advantage of a weighted moving average method, in that more recent observations are assigned larger weights. It reacts faster than the moving average model to changes in the variability of the data. Single exponential smoothing is a procedure in which the forecast for the next period equals the forecast for the prior period, adjusted by an actual amount experienced. Double exponential smoothing may also be used to address trends in the data. (See section 7.7.2, below.)

The smoothing constant a must be determined judgmentally, depending on the sensitivity of the response the model requires. The smaller the value of a, the slower the response. Larger values of *a* cause increasingly quicker reactions in the smoothed (forecast) value. Another difficulty with this method occurs when trying to forecast more than one period ahead. Therefore, this method is designed for and is best used to forecast only one period ahead.

7.6.4   Regression Analysis

This approach to forecasting involves determining the relationships between the dependent and independent variables and representing this relationship in a regression equation. The results of this statistical analysis can be shown in an equation, in tables, or by plotting the regression line for the data set. Regression is a functional relationship between two or more correlated variables that is often empirically determined from data and is used to predict values of one variable when given values of the others. (See section 7.7.3, below.)

Regression equations can be used to predict future requirements or activities based on past data variables input into the regression equations. For example, the variables or drivers can be utilized to predict future events.

7.7   Development of Moving Averages Method

A moving average is a forecast for a future occurrence of an activity based on the most recent occurrences of the activity. The simple moving average model is given by the formula

$$m_t = \frac{1}{n}\sum_{i=0}^{n-1} y_{t-i} = \frac{y_t + y_{t-1} + y_{t-2} + \ldots + y_{t-n+1}}{n} \qquad \{1\}$$

where

   m_t = moving average at time t
   y_t = actual value in period t
   n = number of terms included in the moving average

$$\hat{y}_{t+1} = m_t = \frac{y_t + y_{t-1} + y_{t-2} + \ldots + y_{t-n+1}}{n} \qquad \{3\}$$

or

$$\hat{y}_{t+3} = \frac{\hat{y}_{t+2} + \hat{y}_{t+1} + y_t + y_{t-1} + \ldots + y_{t-n+3}}{n} \qquad \{4\}$$

The simple moving average is the arithmetic mean of the n most recent observations. For computational purposes, the simple moving average can be restated as

$$m_t = m_{t-1} + \frac{y_t + y_{t-n}}{n}$$

Thus, the moving average for three periods in the future is computed using the moving average values for periods 1 and 2 in the future.

7.7.1   Weighted Moving Averages Method

Weighted moving average forecasts are based on utilizing the concepts of the moving average. However, they possibly weight the most recent observations more in the forecasting process. The weighted moving average model is given by the formula:

$$m_t = \sum_{i=0}^{n-1} w_{n-i}\, y_{t-i} = w_n\, y_t + w_{n-1}\, y_{t-1} + \ldots + w_1\, y_{t-n+1}$$

where

$$\sum_{i=0}^{n-1} w_{n-i} = w_n + w_{n-1} + \ldots + w_1 = 1$$

m_t = weighted moving average at time t

y_t = actual value in period t

n = number of terms included in the moving average

w_t = weight on observation for period t

The weighted moving average enables the observations to be weighted such that more importance can be attached to the more recent observations. The weights should be normalized and sum to 1.

7.7.2   Exponential Smoothing Method

In the exponential smoothing method, new forecasts are derived by adjusting the forecasts made for previous periods using their forecast errors. In this way, the forecaster can continually revise the forecast based on past experience. The model has the advantage of a weighted moving average method, in that more recent observations are assigned larger weights. It reacts even faster than the moving average model to changes in the pattern of the data.

The formula for computing the single exponential smoothing value is

$$s_{t+1} = \alpha\, y_t + (1 - \alpha)\, s_t \qquad \{1\}$$

where

s_{t+1} = single exponential smoothing forecast for the next period

s_t = single exponential smoothing forecast for the current period

y_t = actual value in time period t

α = smoothing constant $(0 < \alpha < 1)$

By rewriting s_t in another way as

$$s_{t+1} = s_t + \alpha\, (y_t - s_t) \qquad \{2\}$$

It can be seen that single exponential smoothing is a procedure in which the forecast for the next period equals the forecast for the prior period, adjusted by an amount proportional to the most recent actual occurrence.

$$e_t = y_t - s_t \qquad \{3\}$$

This illustrates how the current forecast error is used to modify the forecast for the next period.

The name "exponential smoothing" comes from the fact that s_t can be expressed as a *weighted average* with exponentially decreasing weights. To see how this is so, you can substitute the expression for s_t and s_{t-1} in the original expression for s_{t+1}.

$$s_t = \alpha \, y_{t-1} + (1-\alpha) \, s_{t-1} \qquad \{4\}$$

$$s_{t-1} = \alpha \, y_{t-2} + (1-\alpha) \, s_{t-2} \qquad \{5\}$$

You can substitute equations {4} and {5} into the original expression for s_{t+1} as follows:

$$s_{t+1} = \alpha \, y_t + (1-\alpha) [\alpha \, y_{t-1} + (1-\alpha) \, s_{t-1}]$$
$$= \alpha \, y_t + \alpha (1-\alpha) \, y_{t-1} + \alpha (1-\alpha)^2 \, y_{t-2} + (1-\alpha)^3 \, s_{t-2} \qquad \{6\}$$

Substituting recursively for s_{t-2}, s_{t-3}, and so on, you obtain

$$s_{t+1} = \alpha \, y_t + \alpha (1-\alpha) \, y_{t-1} + \alpha (1-\alpha)^2 \, y_{t-2} + \ldots$$
$$+ \alpha (1-\alpha)^{t-1} \, y_1 + (1-\alpha)^t \, s_0 \qquad \{7\}$$

or

$$s_{t+1} = \alpha \sum_{k=0}^{t-1} (1-\alpha)^k \, y_{t-k} + (1-\alpha)^t \, s_0 \qquad (0 < \alpha < 1) \qquad \{8\}$$

where

s_0 = initial estimate of the smoothed value

The initial estimate s_0 of the smoothed value can be estimated from historical data by using a simple average of the most recent observations. The receding equation shows that s_{t+1} is a weighted average of $y_t, y_{t-1}, y_{t-2}, \ldots, y_1$ and the initial estimate of s_0. The coefficients of the observations

$\alpha, \alpha(1-\alpha), \alpha(1-\alpha)^2, \ldots, \alpha(1-\alpha)^{t-1}$

are the weights and measure the contribution each observation makes to the most recent estimate. The weights decrease geometrically with increasing k so the most recent values of y_t are given the most weight. Values of y_t more distant in the past, make successively smaller contributions to s_t.

The smoothing constant α must be determined judgmentally, depending on the sensitivity of response the model requires. The smaller the value of α, the slower the response. Larger values of α cause increasingly quicker reactions in the smoothed (forecast) value. Some textbooks recommend that α should lie somewhere between 0.01 and 0.40.

Another difficulty with this method occurs when trying to forecast more than one period ahead. Therefore, this method is designed for and is best used to forecast only one period ahead. Also, an extension of this method is double exponential smoothing, which can be used to address trends in the data.

7.7.3   Regression Analysis Method

This approach to forecasting involves determining the relationships between the dependent and independent variables and representing this relationship in a regression equation. The results of this statistical analysis can be shown in an equation, in tables, or by plotting the regression line for the data set. Regression is a functional relationship between two or more correlated variables that is often empirically determined from data and is used to predict values of one variable when given values of the others.

You can use regression analysis to predict future requirements or activities based on variables input into the regression equations. For example, use the variables or drivers to predict future workloads based on the past relationships between the workload drivers and the resulting work performed.

The general form of the regression equations used in this analysis is shown here:

$$y = \sum_{i=1}^{n} a_i x_i + b,$$

where a_i is the coefficient of each input variable, x_i is the actual value of the input variable, and **b** is the intercept.

You can also use stepwise regression to develop multiple variable equations for forecasting. You can do this by adding new variables to the equation and checking to see if the new equation provides a better forecast. For example, it could reduce the variability around the forecasted value. Stepwise regression uses a statistical test called the F-Test to identify this subset of variables. In the regression analysis, the F-Test would test whether the variance of the variables used in the regression equation is equal to or less than the variance in the original data. Based on the F-Test, variables are either entered if they reduce the variance, or removed from the subset one at a time if they don't until the optimal combination of variables is found. The resulting subset is the best set of variables that significantly reduce the variance and are the most accurate in the predictions or forecasts. Once you have your data in a spreadsheet, such as

MS Excel, you can utilize the built-in statistical functions in MS Excel to easily perform the analysis.

The difficulty in dealing with data is that it is usually missing part of the information you need or that information doesn't exist at all. If data is missing, you may have to generate it through a survey or group expert opinion or select an arbitrary value such as an average between the last value and the next value bracketing the missing data.

It pays to study the available data, i.e., data mining, and determine which methods or approaches it supports. You shouldn't try to capture new data from new sources; this usually requires a great deal of additional time and can make the solution untimely and thus not useful for the current decision.

There is a whole spectrum of statistical analysis tools available from regression, exponential smoothing, and distribution analysis, requiring means and variance estimates.

One good indicator that a process is not in control is the data shows large variability. This can occur in processes throughout the organization from both the demand and production variability. This is a good place to look for out of control processes. This variability should be studied in detail looking of the main cause of source of variability. The analysis would indicate where the variability comes from and what is needed to be tone to minimize this variability.

Chapter 8. Examples of Complex Models—Brewery

8.1   Introduction

In developing an innovative approach to solve a difficult problem, you must separate parts of the problem you feel require different methods. At this point you must clearly understand the objective or objectives. Once you determine the general approach, you need to do the required data analysis/data mining and understand the type of decisions that are to be made. Make a first pass on the particular method required to solve each part of the decision. Analyze the data required for each method in each phase of the problem and determine if it is available in some form or in a database, or if it can be generated easily. This would include data mining, use of surveys, gathering experts and developing subjective expert opinions. At this point, if there are no data available, you will have to select a different method, one that can use subjective data developed by expert opinion methods. Once it is determined that the data is available or can be generated easily, it is a good time to review the data. The data may point to the best decision without going any further and without having to develop a model. If this is the case, the decision can be made and the process terminated. This occurs quite often. It simply indicates that there is an obvious solution and you only need to gather the data to verify it. One quick solution sometimes is by "benchmarking" and selecting the "best practices" for that industry.

If, on the other hand, the decision is not so obvious, we are providing an example in this chapter of how one innovative approach was developed. In the example, a national brewery wants to know how much warehouse space is needed to meet customer demand. There are eleven breweries that supply the wholesaler's product across the entire country. Each brewery is different, with a different customer base and a different product mix.

8.2   The Steps

Step 1. Perform Data Analysis

Perform data analysis and develop demand statistics for service at various levels throughout the company-wide operation. This then indicates that an allocation of resources model is needed, i.e., linear programming. Also, it becomes part of a larger model where we need a great deal of data, including product demand for each brewery, capacity of production for each brewery, and the various trade-offs in the packaging lines. In this phase, we calculate the demand for each product and set a service level of 95 percent availability by simply adding up the product to be stored. These are totaled and indicate that they need three times the available warehouse space to supply all of the products needed where the breweries serve as the distribution centers in the eleven market areas. Thus, we then gather the rest of the data required and solve the linear programming model without the warehouse capacity constraints for each of the breweries. Note: The safety stock must cover the demand and production variability. Then we conducted a separate statistical study to determine how to measure the random variability when the demand was forced to meet production two or three weeks out. This was done and we looked at the 95 percent service level on all products, noting we did not have the warehouse space to do this. This required us to prioritize the products so we had 95 percent safety stock on a few prime products, depending upon their priority. We then ran the linear programming model to determine how much of the product demand could be met as an initial solution and did sensitivity analysis to test and verify the solutions.

In summary, in Step 1 we selected the primary allocation of resources model, i.e., linear programming. But to use this approach, we had to do an extensive statistical study on product demand and production variability to get an idea of the safety stock required. Also, we had to prioritize the products and supply the minimum service levels for each of the products at each brewery.

Step 2. Solve the Linear Programming Model

Once the safety stock and product priority were set, we could then determine the slate of products and the amount that could optimally be produced. This then provided us with the production requirements at each brewery on a weekly basis. While this gave us a weekly demand requirement for each of the breweries, we were not sure we could schedule these products through the breweries with their current levels of production. We had to develop a simulation model to determine the detailed shift scheduling of production through the brewery. At this time we could see we needed a broader application capability approach and the simulation model would accomplish this.

Step 3. Do the actual scheduling with the simulation program

We developed a simulation program for each brewery on a three-shift basis for seven days per week. Such models were developed for each brewery and scheduled each shift from Monday to Sunday. This approach allowed packaging lines constraints on a shift basis each day of each week. This model was exercised a number of times by sampling the demand distributions, and then recorded. We were then able to determine the days of the week and the weeks of the year to identify the warehouse bottlenecks and plan the warehouses' needs throughout the year.

To summarize, we needed to analyze the data and to review the process of developing innovative approaches. The available data, the detail required for the decision and the timeliness, and understanding the methods to be applied were all part of the process.

8.3   Development of Models

Key components of model development are described below.

1. Define: We look at the data, the scope of the decision to be made and when it needs to be made, and identify the detailed data required to make this decision. This includes examining the scope and the type of answer required. We can then select an approach that will provide the answers we need. We look at each phase of the analysis, selecting a variety of methods to cover each phase and how the data flows through the model.

2. Selection of methods for decision making: First comes the development of data through data mining and evaluating the available databases. Sometimes, the actual data is historical data and the usual statistics can be used. Other times, the actual data is not available and must be developed as subjective data. Actual data can be analyzed by a variety of standard statistical methods by studying the variability and the use of regression analysis when appropriate. For subjective data or expert opinions and group consensus, we must look for proactive methods, such as NGT, SPAN, brainstorming and brainwriting.

3. Model adjustment: It's also important to select the methods that the decision maker can understand and will use. This is probably the most important part of the process. This process is shown below in Figure 8.1.

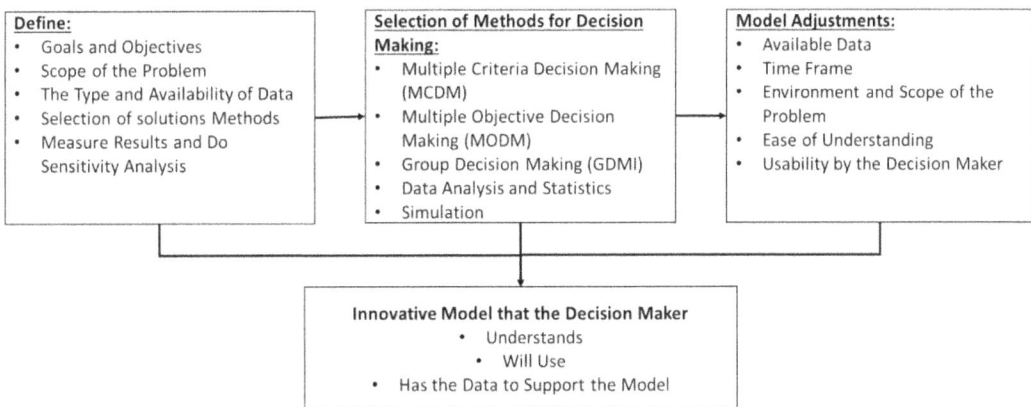

| Define:
 • Goals and Objectives
 • Scope of the Problem
 • The Type and Availability of Data
 • Selection of solutions Methods
 • Measure Results and Do Sensitivity Analysis | Selection of Methods for Decision Making:
 • Multiple Criteria Decision Making (MCDM)
 • Multiple Objective Decision Making (MODM)
 • Group Decision Making (GDMI)
 • Data Analysis and Statistics
 • Simulation | Model Adjustments:
 • Available Data
 • Time Frame
 • Environment and Scope of the Problem
 • Ease of Understanding
 • Usability by the Decision Maker |

Innovative Model that the Decision Maker
• Understands
• Will Use
• Has the Data to Support the Model

Figure 8.1 Decision Model Development Process

The data, its form, and availability dictate how we approach selecting methods and what analysis is performed in solving the problem. This involves data mining and reviewing all sources of information and data. Sometimes, it exists in related databases that were developed for other uses and can be reformatted for our purposes. Also, gathering knowledgeable people and getting information based on their experiences and opinions is very helpful.

There are two types of data, statistical or historical data, and subjective or future data, which are generated by group consensus or expert opinions. Remember that there are special approaches that can be used to accomplish this, which were discussed in previous chapters.

The knowledge of methods based on education and experience and their application on other problems helps individuals select the solution approach. The following are some of the problems we faced in the brewery model. Some of the steps necessary to develop a decision model are stated below.

- Applying the methods to the problem of how much inventory was needed:
    o Adapting safety stock calculations to meet customer demand. This required identifying the point of true variability in order to calculate safety stock instead of simply looking at demand variability.
    o Adapting the use of methods to different levels of organizational usage, e.g., using the concept of activity relationship diagrams from the factory floor to strategic planning by corporate executives.
    o Using methods in one environment and applying them to another environment, e.g., flexible manufacturing applied to flexible warehousing.
    o Making problems manageable based on data aggregation methods, i.e., using market baskets to significantly reduce the model size and maintain environmental operation.
- Adding features to existing methods to provide additional insight into problems and their solutions, e.g., taking existing ranking methods and adding structured sensitivity analysis to provide insights into the variability of solutions.
- Understanding the breadth of available methods to truly model the environment, e.g., using multiple objective decision making vs. linear programming or using statistical methods or simulation.

We then need to determine the type of analysis needed for each part of the decision process.

8.4   Approach to the Brewery Model

Once you determine the general approach and method, and the required data analysis (subjective, objective), you can then structure your decision model. The following steps were used to build the model.

1. Start with the linear programming (LP) model and identify the data needed as shown in Figure 8.2. This required an analysis of the demand data. At this point, we set the critical products with average demand plus a safety stock at 95 percent satisfaction and totaled it up. We discovered we needed three times the available warehouse space. We then set up and solved a LP model and determined how much we could supply with no constraints on the warehouse capacity.

Linear Programming Model	Demand
	Capacity
	Trade-off of Resources

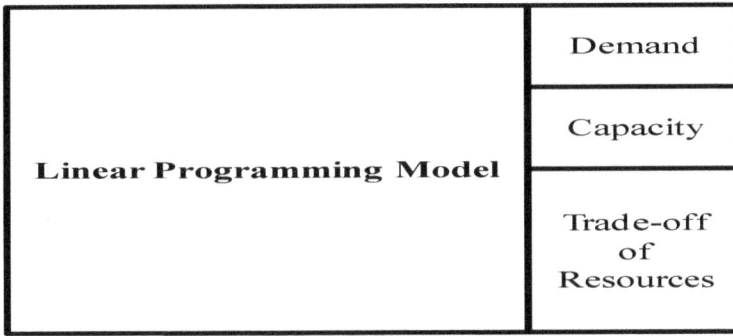

Figure 8.2 Structure of Linear Programming Model

2. We then put warehouse capacity in and noted which products were produced (arbitrarily) and we couldn't supply all the demand. We then had to prioritize the products and identify the minimum amount of product that was satisfactory. (This changed for each product, for each region.)

3. The safety stock calculation required considering both demand and production variability. We realized that LP solves for one time period by week or could include all weeks, which resulted in a very large model. Also, some parts of the model were nonlinear (e.g., scheduling shifts) and had integer requirements.

4. The results of the LP model that had a time period of a week were used to structure a simulation so we could track production and delivery by shift, by day, with constraints determined by the LP model on which products or size best utilized the packaging equipment and optimized product throughput.

5. We then did a great deal of sensitivity analysis to explore the options, cost them out, and see how best to integrate them into the current operation.

This brewery warehouse study required an innovative approach, since there was no single method that could solve the problem. Thus, we had to construct a combined method (see Figure 8.3) to solve the problem. It included:

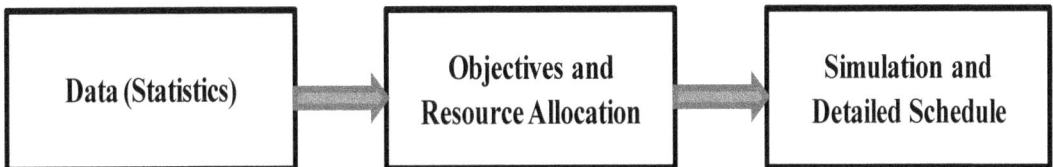

| Data (Statistics) | → | Objectives and Resource Allocation | → | Simulation and Detailed Schedule |

Figure 8.3 Key Elements of the Detailed Operating Model

1. We completed a statistical analysis of demand data and production variability to ensure the safety stock and provide the desired service level (statistics) for the ranked importance of the products (MADM).

2. We then had to allocate the product to utilize all of the production and distribution capacities (linear programming).

3. This linear programming solution was used for a fixed time period of one week.

4. This problem required a daily detailed operating model that was not linear. Thus, simulation was used to represent the actual environment on a shift, day, and week and adjusted seasonally.

This study is described in detail in an eBook, *Warehouse and Inventory Level Optimization*, published by the authors.

Chapter 9. Value-Based Budgeting

9.1   Introduction

In this class of budgeting problems, we developed a capability called value-based budgeting was developed. This capability is a budgeting approach that is different than zero-based budgeting, the traditional all or nothing approach to budgeting, or the salami slice approach to cutting budgets. The value-based budgeting approach was developed to assist management in a much more logical budgeting approach for allocating scarce resources.

Value based-budgeting provides a basic structure of which projects can be identified, measured, and funded based on their overall contribution to the established goals of the organization. Based on the project's overall consensus ranking and score in the list of projects, a proportion of the total resources (a percentage) is earned by each project or function. Projects or functions are then funded to either their minimum or maximum requirement based on this earned value and the amount of available resources. If the earned resources are less than the minimum level of support required, no additional resources are allocated. If a project earns more than the minimum resource requirement, the additional resources are proportionally assigned. If projects earn more than their maximum funding level, the projects are then funded to the maximum level for the project. Then as budgets change, the minimum and maximum levels are funded and the cuts or plus ups in the middle are made in proportion to their value. This value is the cardinal value of the rank score, which is an output of the technique for order of preference by similarity to ideal solution (TOPSIS) ranking methodology.

If projects are funded and resource levels change, percentage cuts without regard to real needs (the salami slice) can be counterproductive to an efficient utilization of dollars and manpower. This approach provides the framework for making difficult resource allocation decisions based on total organizational needs and has the capability to integrate both manpower and dollars. It is user-friendly, accountable to dynamic real-world situational changes, sensitive to "what-if" analysis, and provides a funding scenario consistent with the decision process.

This capability is described in more detail through an application developed for a military base. The methodology was programmed into a user-friendly tool that enabled dynamic changes to budgeting based on changes to the installation's funding. The capabilities and examples are described below. This approach is just as valid for the corporate world and any other organization that has a limited budget.

9.2   Resource Management Decision Support Method

The resource management system is a decision making method used across the activities throughout an organization to allocate available resources based on mission prioritization. This approach is a prioritization tool that aids the user in prioritizing the missions within an activity. It is also a budgeting tool that aids the user in allocating available resources to each mission, and enabling the user the ability to do what-if analysis for different budgeting scenarios. The approach as a whole provides the user with the capability to best allocate the available resources for each of the missions within an activity.

The approach simplifies and standardizes the prioritization and budgeting process by:

1. Lessening the amount of time that is currently spent making tough prioritization and budget allocation decisions.
2. Establishing, tracking, and validating objective decisions based on established criteria.
3. Performing what-if analysis with the available resources to determine the best possible budget allocation scheme.
4. Providing an approach able to handle quickly up-to-date funding changes.
5. Standardizing components of the budgeting process from year-to-year.

The following section explains how it works.

9.2.1   Data Used in the System

The input data contains information about the project and the criteria utilized for the prioritization. Various pieces of information are captured in this approach to make it a comprehensive budgeting and planning approach. This information was stored in a database for decision making and historical reference. Although specifics may change based on your own organization's needs, the capabilities provide a sound way to make good prioritization and budgeting decisions.

9.2.2   Project Data

A simple set of project data is shown below. This data is comprised of decision criteria used to prioritize the project and some additional budgeting information. A group of corporate executives met to discuss and develop the decision criteria used in the prioritization process. These decision criteria reflected the goals and objectives of the organization.

Budget information was captured in regards to each of the projects. Key pieces of data were the minimum cost and the maximum funding for each of the projects. This data is shown below in the following table, along with the decision criteria.

Table 9.1 Project Data

Project Name	Revenue	Strategic Value	Minimum Cost	Number of Business Units Impacted	Technical Difficulty	Probability of Success	Maximum Cost
Project 1	$300,000	5	$50,000	8	1	95%	$150,000
Project 2	$1,000,000	5	$500,000	10	3	75%	$100,000
Project 3	$1,250,000	4	$600,000	6	4	60%	$200,000
Project 4	$700,000	4	$100,000	8	2	90%	$60,000
Project 5	$850,000	3	$300,000	5	5	60%	$100,000
Project 6	$150,000	2	$30,000	3	1	90%	$700,000
Project 7	$650,000	2	$100,000	3	3	70%	$400,000
Project 8	$250,000	2	$50,000	2	2	90%	$650,000

Brief definitions of the decision criteria are given below.

- Revenue: The anticipated revenue over a two-year time frame
- Strategic value: This represents the strategic importance of the project to the company. This is scored on a scale from 1 through 5, where 1 is of little strategic value, and 5 is significant strategic value.
- Minimum cost: This is the minimum expenditure to complete the project. Cost is used in budgeting, but it is also an important criterion used to ensure the company's cash flow when selecting projects.
- Number of business units impacted: This criterion represents the breadth of the project's impact. It contributes less to the company's goals if it impacts a smaller number of business units rather than a larger number of business units.
- Technical difficulty: This criterion captures the decision makers' feelings about how difficult it will be to accomplish the project. This is scored on a scale from 1 through 5, where 1 is little difficulty, and 5 is significant technical difficulty.
- Probability of success: This criterion captures the assessed risk of the project in terms of whether it can be completed successfully. The executives would like to invest in projects with a higher chance of success.

9.3   Decision Criteria Weighting

This approach allows the user to directly choose the relevant criteria weight or use a pairwise comparison weighting technique, or to see whether each criterion is maximized or minimized.

For the direct entry of weights, the decision maker enters a value for each of the criteria. These weights are normalized so the weights of the criteria sum to one. For example, if four criteria are weighted as (2, 3, 1, 4) the resulting weights are (0.2, 0.3, 0.1, 0.4).

This also shows whether a criterion is a *cost*, or minimized, so that a smaller score is a better score, or whether it is a *benefit*, or maximized, so that a larger score is a better score. The methodology used for the ranking, TOPSIS, uses this information in its computations to form a best case solution and a worst case solution. This is a strength of the methodology: criteria evaluations can be entered in "real-world" terms that are intuitive to the decision maker.

Table 9.2 Decision Matrix with Budgeting Information

Input Weights	10	7	9	5	6	8	
Weights	22%	16%	20%	11%	13%	18%	
	BENEFIT	BENEFIT	COST	BENEFIT	COST	BENEFIT	
Project Name	Revenue	Strategic Value	Minimum Cost	Number of Business Units Impacted	Technical Difficulty	Probability of Success	Maximum Cost
Project 1	$300,000	5	$50,000	8	1	95%	$150,000
Project 2	$1,000,000	5	$500,000	10	3	75%	$100,000
Project 3	$1,250,000	4	$600,000	6	4	60%	$200,000
Project 4	$700,000	4	$100,000	8	2	90%	$60,000
Project 5	$850,000	3	$300,000	5	5	60%	$100,000
Project 6	$150,000	2	$30,000	3	1	90%	$700,000
Project 7	$650,000	2	$100,000	3	3	70%	$400,000
Project 8	$250,000	2	$50,000	2	2	90%	$650,000

9.4   Project Ranking

This section ranks each project on the basis of the score obtained through the TOPSIS algorithmic ranking process. This score is the closeness of that criterion to the best possible solution and it is an indisputable preference order of items. The score resulting from the ranking process is used to generate the rank of each of the projects. This score is determined from the values entered for each of the criteria and the weighting scheme determined from the weights. The user can do what-if analysis for the prioritization of the missions by running the ranking algorithm with different sets of weights for the criteria. This allows the decision maker the ability to determine the best possible prioritization based on the goals and objectives of the organization.

Table 9.3 Project Ranking

Input Weights	10	7	9	5	6	8			
Weights	22%	16%	20%	11%	13%	18%			
	BENEFIT	BENEFIT	COST	BENEFIT	COST	BENEFIT			
Project Name	Revenue	Strategic Value	Minimum Cost	Number of Business Units Impacted	Technical Difficulty	Probability of Success	Maximum Cost	Score	Rank
Project 4	$700,000	4	$100,000	8	2	90%	$150,000	0.6942	1
Project 1	$300,000	5	$50,000	8	1	95%	$100,000	0.6099	2
Project 7	$650,000	2	$100,000	3	3	70%	$200,000	0.5734	3
Project 6	$150,000	2	$30,000	3	1	90%	$60,000	0.5303	4
Project 8	$250,000	2	$50,000	2	2	90%	$100,000	0.5238	5
Project 2	$1,000,000	5	$500,000	10	3	75%	$700,000	0.5033	6
Project 5	$850,000	3	$300,000	5	5	60%	$400,000	0.4836	7
Project 3	$1,250,000	4	$600,000	6	4	60%	$650,000	0.4572	8

9.5 Budget Allocation

The approach suggests three different methods to allocate funds. The first method is the criteria allocation option, the second method is the slice of minimum requirements option, and the third option is the individual adjustment of funding.

9.5.1 Criteria Allocation Option

The approach calculates a criteria-based prioritization-funding scheme for the missions in each program. This allocation scheme is based on the *score* resulting from the prioritization. This *score* is used to determine a dollar value associated with each mission. This dollar value is compared to the minimum and maximum requirements of the project to allocate value-based funds to the mission.

The algorithm for the value-based budgeting methodology is shown below:

CASE 1: budget ≤ sum of minimum required
CASE 2: sum of minimum required < budget < sum of total required

allocate the minimum required, scored amount, or total required, starting from the top of the ranked list of projects

While (budget > 0)

For projects ranked first to last do the following:

1. Allocate the scored amount to the project, but do not exceed the total required and meet at least the minimum required.
2. Reduce the budget by the amount allocated.
3. If the budget = 0, stop.
4. If (budget > 0), then
5. New budget = original budget – funds for projects at total required
6. Re-compute a new scored amount with this new budget for all projects between the minimum and maximum required.

Table 9.4 Budget Allocation

Budget $1,100,000

Project Name	Ranked Score	Rank	Minimum Cost	Maximum Cost	Budget % from Score	Allocated Budget	Initial Funding	Budget Remaining	Final Funding	
Project 4	0.6942	1	$100,000	$150,000	15.86%	$174,515	$150,000	$950,000	$150,000	
Project 1	0.6099	2	$50,000	$100,000	13.94%	$153,308	$100,000	$850,000	$100,000	
Project 7	0.5734	3	$100,000	$200,000	13.10%	$144,149	$144,149	$705,851	$190,000	***
Project 6	0.5303	4	$30,000	$60,000	12.12%	$133,321	$60,000	$645,851	$60,000	
Project 8	0.5238	5	$50,000	$100,000	11.97%	$131,682	$100,000	$545,851	$100,000	
Project 2	0.5033	6	$500,000	$700,000	11.50%	$126,523	$500,000	$45,851	$500,000	
Project 5	0.4836	7	$300,000	$400,000	11.05%	$121,578	$0	$45,851	$0	
Project 3	0.4572	8	$600,000	$650,000	10.45%	$114,925	$0	$45,851	$0	
	4.3758					Total	$1,054,149		$1,100,000	

The table shows the amount remaining after meeting the required minimum of several projects. No funds were allocated to projects 5 and 3 because we could not meet the minimum and they were ranked last.

9.5.2   Slice of Minimum Requirements

Many organizations use a process called the slice of minimum requirements. Here, the company simply reduces the amount of funds allocated to a project based on a given percentage. Many times all projects are funded; however, all must then take a percent budget cut. This level will be used to adjust ALL of the minimum requirements for each project funded by that program. This method, however, can have significant impacts on the ability to successfully complete projects or programs.

9.5.3   Individual Funding Level Options.

Even if individuals use one of the methods above, they may want to adjust the funding levels individually for each project or a number of projects. It is beneficial to use the other two methods described above to provide a different perspective on allocating budgets. It may be that a combination of methods is useful from an overall budgeting perspective to arrive at a well-analyzed funding scenario.

9.6   Summary

This study provides a view of a decision science-based method to allocate funds to projects within an organization and link that funding to meeting corporate objectives. The value-based budgeting capability was developed as an alternative to the traditional all or nothing approach to budgeting, or the salami slice approach to cutting budgets. It was developed to give management a much more logical budgeting approach for allocating scarce resources.

Chapter 10. Logistics Pipeline Analysis Example

10.1 Introduction

Following is an example of a system that has been developed that focuses on the metrics of an organization. This system was based on work done for the Department of Defense, but it is equally applicable to large distribution systems of sizable commercial companies. It can be utilized on an ongoing analysis capability, where users can connect to data and perform a system analysis on their own.

The model is based on metrics developed from organizational goals that are then used to assess the performance of the organization. Once metrics are established and tracked, decisions are evident. Users can review organizational performance and then make decisions on how to improve their operations. The metrics themselves and tracking of the metrics are quite valuable to the organization. Many times metrics are developed in a production operation, e.g., a packaging line, part specifications, etc. quality control procedures are used to track the production of an item and adjustments are made to keep items within the acceptable tolerances. This example is the product analysis concept that is used to measure and track the functional activities within the organization. In the context of this example, functional activities are tracked rather than product specifications. These metrics capture and track the functional operation of an organization at all levels, based on attaining the goals and objectives of the organization. This approach is suitable and beneficial for a variety of applications in all organizations. Developing decision models with metrics such as this can be extremely valuable in understanding and improving the operating environment of the organization.

Additionally, the source data for these models are approximately 80 million records from numerous Department of Defense databases. This information was extracted and summarized and made available to users on personnel computers. With the type of technology available today, this is all possible, where previously it was not.

10.2 Example of Metrics System—Logistics Pipeline Analyzer (LPA) Automated System

The purpose of the logistics pipeline analyzer (LPLA) was to provide logistics and operational managers and analysts with an automated, user-friendly tool that facilitates analyses of the various parts and logistic materiel (military materials and equipment), such as the in-transit parts, in-process orders, returns/redistribution of parts, and the disposal/reutilization of parts and systems pipeline. See Figure 10.1.

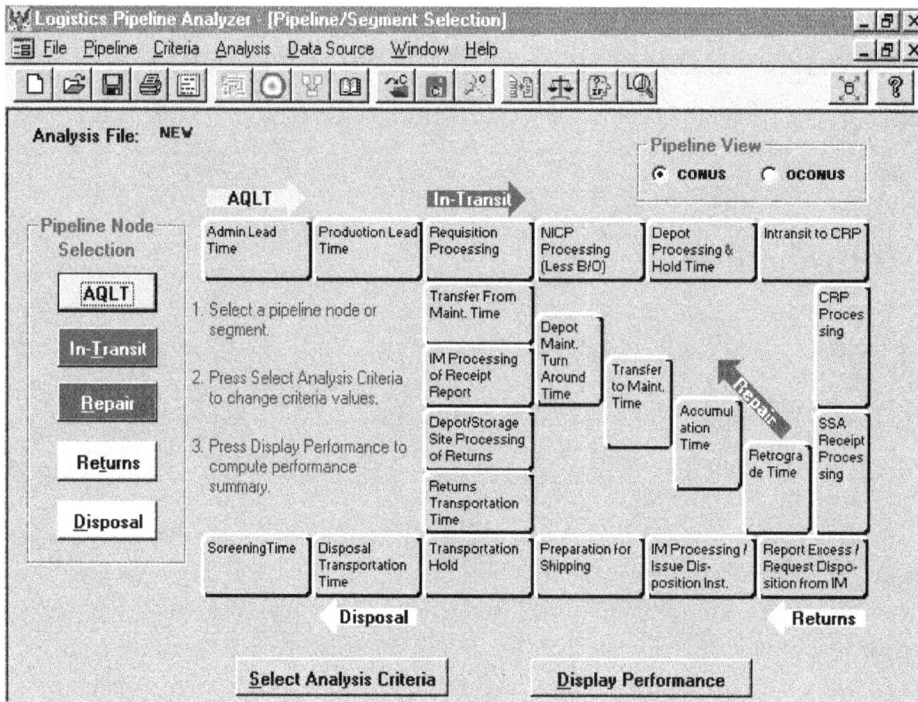

Figure 10.1 Logistics Pipeline Analyzer (LPA)

The logistics pipeline tracks inventory in acquisition and production, in storage, in maintenance, and in transit (transportation) from the factory to the ultimate consumer. It also includes inventory returned from the consumer for redistribution and reutilization and disposal. A number of army databases and associated data analysis and display capabilities are used in providing the visibility to analyze this pipeline. Prior to this system, numerous reports were available from a large number of databases. They were of limited value in assisting logistics managers and analysts in analyzing the army's total logistics pipeline because they were scattered throughout the army and not quick to obtain. Individually, these reports did not provide a complete picture of each segment of the pipeline. Collectively, the reports were difficult to use since they did not have a standard format or consistent time period. As a result, the manager or analyst had little flexibility in analyzing and identifying potential pipeline problems. There was no single automated tool to integrate all of the different databases for the logistician or analyst who consolidates and integrates the information available.

The LPA was developed as an automated tool that provides more meaningful management information in analyzing the performance of the army's total logistics parts and weapon systems pipeline. The LPA provides an automated management tool for tactical/operational staff, and for senior leadership to more easily analyze the supply, maintenance, transportation, and disposal segments of the army's logistics pipelines. The analyzer provides the capability to identify "cause and effect" relationships, such that specific problem areas in the pipelines can be identified as areas for immediate corrective action or seen as opportunities for new or revised business practice concept development and testing.

10.3 Objectives of the Logistics Pipeline Analyzer

The objectives of the logistics pipeline analyzer were:

1. Establish mechanisms to capture information that enables logistic managers to evaluate and continuously improve pipeline performance.
2. Enhance weapon system management by providing an analysis tool of logistic pipelines.
3. Enhance visibility of resource information to improve the decision making process.
4. Improve the use of resources (i.e., cost) that will facilitate decision making in a cost-service tradeoff.
5. Improve the integration and coordination of the management of the various weapon system pipelines and their segments by:
   a. Determining past performance and forecasting future performance.
   b. Comparing actual performance against established standards.
   c. Performing what if analysis.
   d. Tailoring pipeline strategies and systems management to meet the specific needs of different customer communities.

The logistics pipeline is divided into four major segments. Each of these segments has additional segments within it to further define the pipeline. Following is a brief description of the DOD logistics pipeline.

In-process pipeline: This pipeline is composed of processes that occur when requirements are placed on order from DOD vendors and not yet shipped, when assets are in repair at depot-level organic or commercial repair facilities, and when assets are in repair at intermediate repair facilities. Inherent in these pipeline segments are delays associated with the processing of procurement/repair orders and with the actual production or depot repair operation. By definition, management of the in-process pipelines involves other functions, such as acquisition and maintenance.

In-transit pipeline: This pipeline is composed of the movement of the item once it is in the system and on its way to its destination. There are multiple steps in this process, both from a record keeping and from positioning stocks. For the LPA, the in-transit pipeline is composed of installation processing time, inventory control processing (ICP) (fewer backorders) time, depot processing and hold time, in-transit to a central receiving point time (CRP), CRP processing time, and supply support activity (SSA) receipt processing time segments. These time segments include both supply and transportation segments.

Returns/redistribution pipeline: This pipeline is composed of those processes associated with the actual movement or transportation of materiel returned from army customers to a wholesale supply activity. The returned materiel may be redistributed to other DOD customers, or if it is in an unserviceable condition, it may be scheduled for repair and stored until required.

Disposal/reutilization pipeline: This pipeline is composed of those processes associated with the disposal of materiel determined to be surplus to DOD needs or of materiel determined to be uneconomically repairable or only having scrap value. By definition it must be processed through a Defense Reutilization and Marketing Office (DRMO) for screening for possible reutilization within DOD and other designated agencies. Upon completion of screening it may be disposed of by the DRMO. Depending on the materiel, it may require demilitarization prior to disposal.

10.4   System Structure

Performance tracking and analysis was provided to users at all levels of the organization to give them the ability to better manage the logistics pipeline. Significant resources are expended in materiel management for the DOD. The identification and improvement of any and all of the pipelines and pipeline segments provide significant opportunities in cost reductions and improved customer service. The LPA has been designed to provide users at all levels with the ability to analyze and assess logistics performance at each of the stages of logistics management. By clearly understanding current performance, historical performance, and performance trends, management is able to focus their efforts on areas where performance can be improved.

One of the key characteristics of the LPA system is its flexibility. The LPA system has been designed to accommodate management and management analysis at all levels. Performance summary information can be rolled up, for example, for a subordinate command, or can be analyzed on an individual national stock numbers (NSN) basis.

Another important characteristic of the LPA system is its ability to support the detail that was used to generate the various system performance calculations. Certain performance statistics can be generated for a selected group of NSNs. Results may appear reasonable or appear to be out of the ordinary. The LPA system provides the back-up detail that can be used to support the results generated by the system. Many times, a "bottom line" performance statistic may not tell the entire story. In some cases, where lead times may appear to be high, the back-up detail may show that extenuating circumstances surrounded a specific NSN. Other times, there may be no extenuating circumstances, and the conclusion may be that this is an area that needs additional attention.

Providing the ability for all levels of management to view and analyze performance aids in identifying performance improvement opportunities. Business process enhancements can be identified and suggested to reduce the resource investment in the pipeline by reducing the time and size of the pipeline functions. The LPA system provides the analysis capabilities to better manage costs and monitor performance leading to increased responsiveness to customer requirements and improvements in the bottom line cost of logistics operations.

The following shows an example of the analysis capabilities provided in the LPA system. The user first selects the pipeline segment to analyze. In this example, the user selects the acquisition lead time pipeline (AQLT) segment (see Figure 10.2). Users then select the command, weapon system, supply class, support category, priority group, and review period for the analysis. The available selection criteria are meaningful to the individual managing the item for the army. Figure 10.2 shows the analysis criteria used in this example. These criteria are the following:

command = all army

weapon system = all weapon systems

supply class = all (II, III(P), IV and IX) – all essentiality codes, repairable, all sources

support category = "blank"

priority group = routine

review period = 24 months

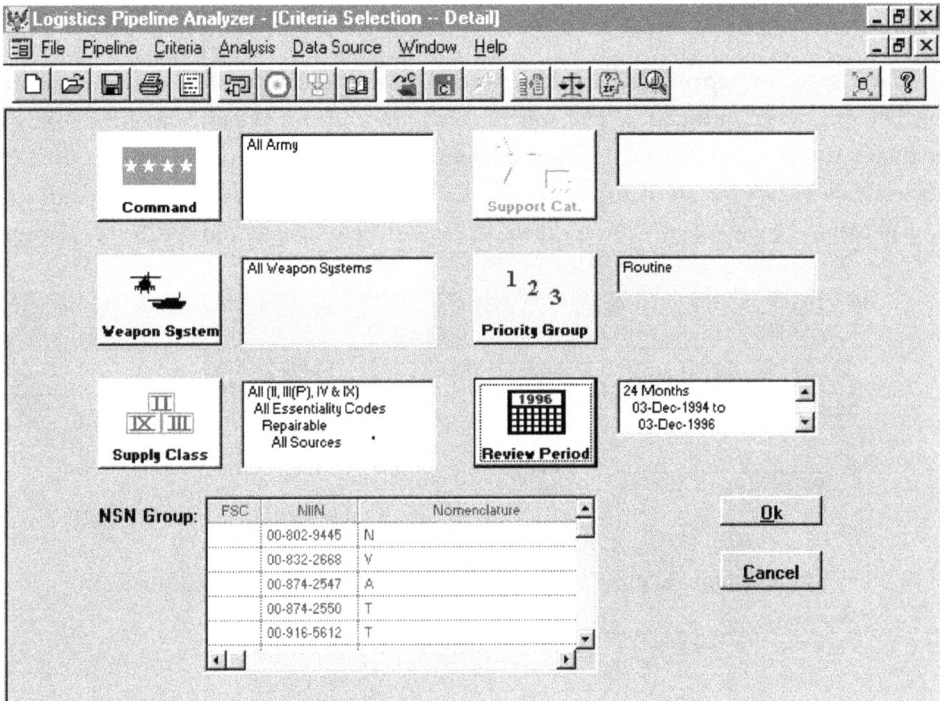

Figure 10.2 Criteria Selection Screen

Performance Tracking

The LPA provides the ability to perform performance tracking using two primary representations of the NSN (national stock number) data. The first group of performance statistics tracks the lead time associated with a specific NSN. The second group of performance statistics tracks the dollar investment value of an NSN as associated with the lead times and the item costs. Any of the defined pipelines or pipeline segments can be selected for the analysis. Detailed data is maintained for each of the NSNs supporting the Abrams M1 Tank or the Apache Helicopter. This information can be grouped using any variety of criteria, including commands, supply class, essentiality, reparability, supply source, support category, and priority group. This information is maintained on a time series basis such that a specific period of time can be viewed for the selected grouping of NSNs. The basic structure of the LPA provides the building blocks and flexibility for user performance analysis specifically supporting the manager's requirements. Performance statistics can be generated for any cut of data supported by the LPA.

Examples of some of the LPA's basic performance analysis capabilities for performance tracking for individual or a group of NSNs are listed below:

- On a monthly, quarterly, yearly, or bi-yearly basis
- By command, subcommand, or supply source
- Based on specific characteristics associated with an NSN, such as supply class, reparability, essentiality, priority group, or support category
- Performance compared to command goals

These types of capabilities provide the user with the ability to analyze and manage areas that they can directly influence. The specific analyses performed can enable the user to identify and highlight opportunity areas for improvement. The example shown in Figure 10.3 shows the performance values for all of the NSNs in the selected criteria group. This includes the actual and forecasted processing time in months, the investment values, and the NSN quantities.

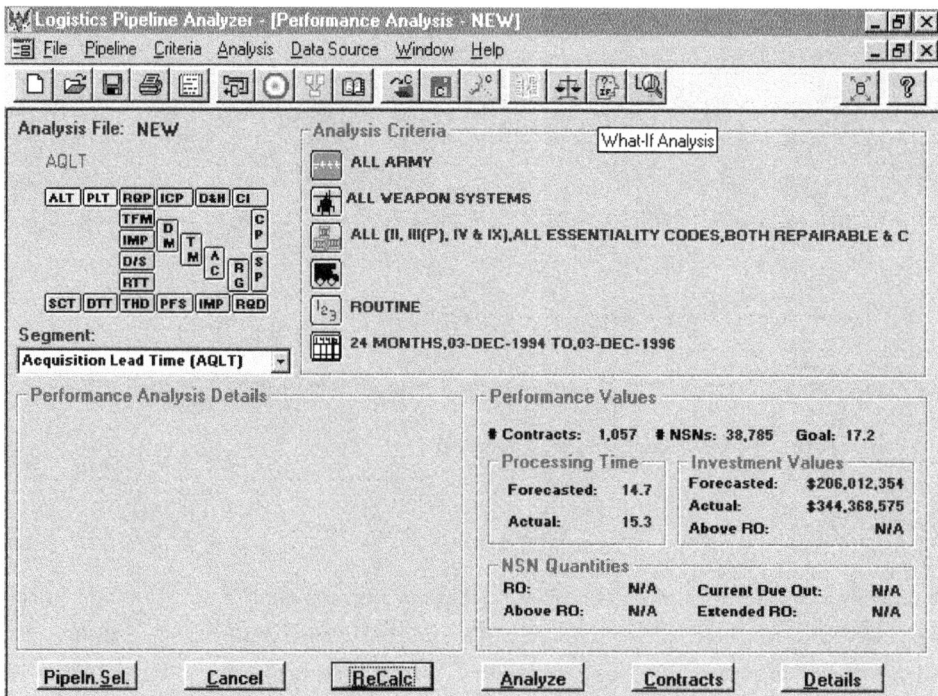

Figure 10.3 Performance Values of All the NSNs in the Selected Criteria Group

Enhanced Analysis

The performance analysis capability provides a view of some or all of the NSNs managed by the various levels of the organization. The base performance analysis capability provides the starting point for user analyses. The analysis capabilities discussed below provide additional techniques available to further analyze the NSN data tracked with the LPA.

Compare Analysis

The compare analysis provided by the LPA enables the user with the ability to compare the performance of one grouping of NSNs against another grouping of NSNs or individual NSN(s). The analytical capabilities are the same as those provided with the basic performance analysis; however, this capability can be used to perform side-by-side comparisons of the various cases. Figure 10.4 shows an example of the compare analysis, where all of the same analysis criteria have been selected, except for the priority, which is IPG I. IPG I denotes a higher level ordering priority for a given NSN.

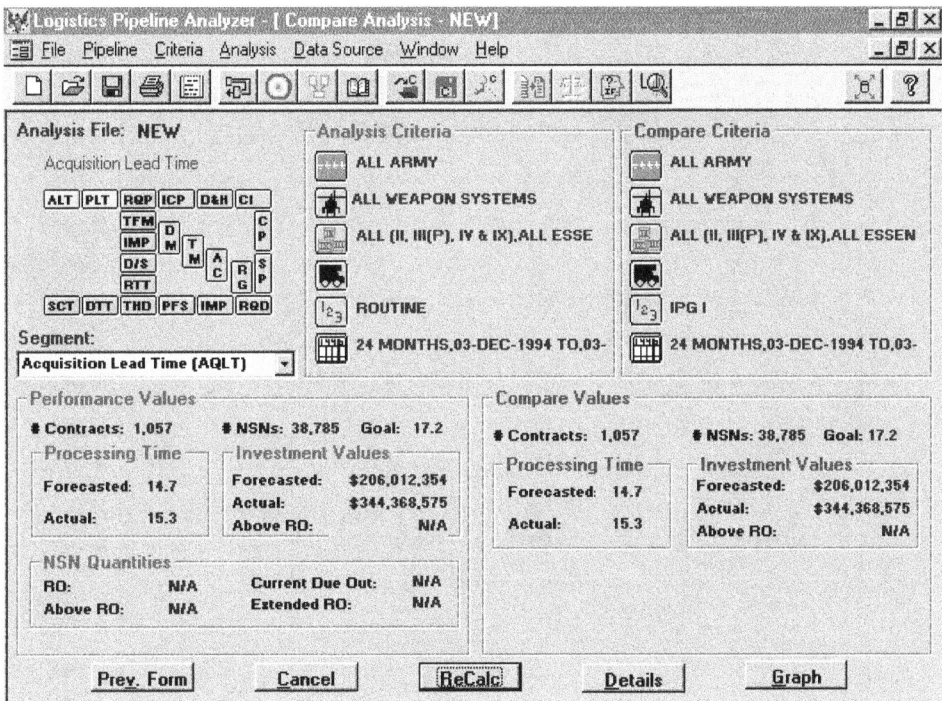

Figure 10.4 Example of the LPA Compare Analysis

For example, an item manager may generate a performance summary associated with the specific NSNs he or she manages. In generating the performance statistics, the user may note that the lead time exceeds the command lead time goal for a specific pipeline by a number of months. The user can then perform a compare analysis of the total group of NSNs to various individual NSNs to determine which of the NSNs appear to be out of tolerance. Once the out-of-tolerance NSNs are identified, the user can then decide whether those specific NSNs require additional attention. If, for example, the NSNs out of tolerance constitute a large investment, i.e., a higher dollar value or large volume, the user can then initiate management procedures that attempt to reduce the lead times. If the NSNs out of tolerance constitute a smaller investment, the item manager may decide to focus attention in other areas.

There are numerous types of compare analyses that can be performed with the LPA. These analyses can be used to better understand operating performance, to identify and assess potential areas of opportunity for improvement, and to influence operating changes.

Trend Analysis

The trend analysis within the LPA provides another powerful analysis capability that can be used to identify areas of potential operating improvements. Trend analysis can be used to graphically analyze past historical performance and project future performance based on past history. Areas where there have been increases or decreases in performance can be identified with this capability. An example of the LPA trend analysis capability is shown in Figure 10.5. The information extracted by the system is summarized either by month or by quarter.

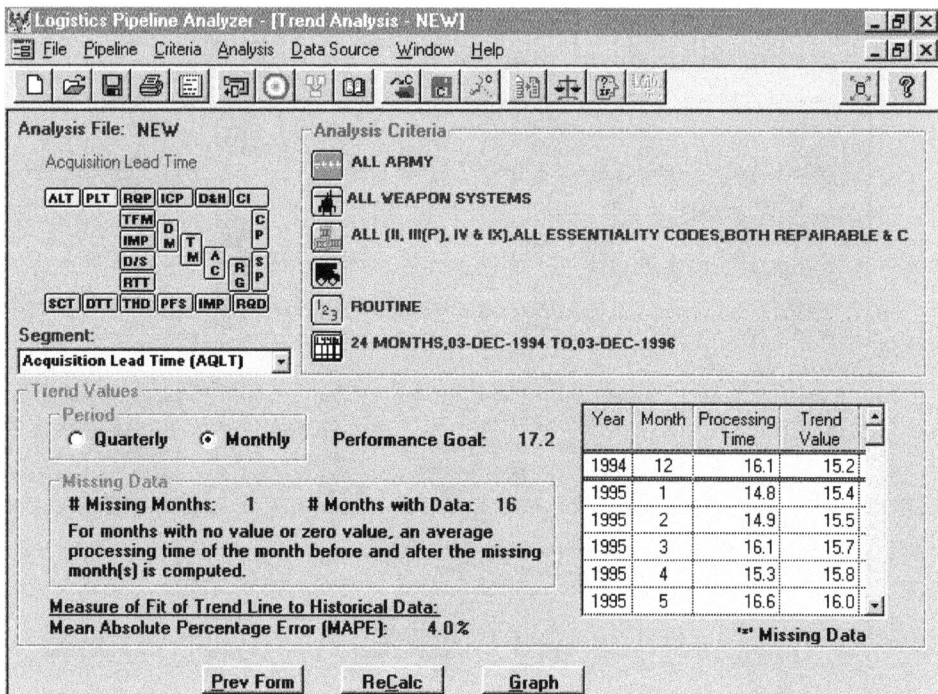

Figure 10.5 Example of LPA Trend Analysis

For example, the user may generate a performance summary for a selected group of NSNs over a period of time. The user can then generate a trend analysis to determine whether the past performance and trend appear to be constant, increasing, or decreasing. From this, the user may identify an increase in lead times over the given time period and determine that if the trend continues, lead times for the group of NSNs may continue to increase over the next six months. Based on the pipeline that is being analyzed, the user may want to perform additional analyses on individual pipeline segments. If specific pipeline segments appear to be causing the increases, further review into operating procedures, changes in policy, etc. may be conducted to identify the reasons for the increases and determine what factors can be controlled to reverse the trend. The user may also perform additional analysis on a breakdown or subgrouping of the NSNs to determine whether or not there are certain NSNs influencing the trend. This also can lead to the identification of areas to focus improvement efforts.

What If Analysis

The what if analysis capability of the LPA enables the user to determine the impact of changes in lead times on the investment in the pipeline. Investment values calculated by the LPA system use the lead times and the unit price of an item to determine the dollar days associated with an NSN. These performance values are intended to represent a dollar figure tied to a DOD resource investment. Certain items may be of low dollar value and have a high volume and lead time, but, in essence, represent a minimal commitment of resources associated with the item. On the other hand, there may be high dollar items, requiring a large dollar investment, which may have lead times shorter than the command goals. If the lead times were reduced, it could significantly impact the investment in the pipeline. The what if analysis capability is designed to perform an analysis such as this. Lead times can be changes for individual pipeline segments within a pipeline and the resulting investment value calculated. Figure 10.6 shows an example of the LPA what if analysis capability. This provides the user with the capability to assess the lead time performance and policies, and determine the areas that can affect the investment in the pipeline most greatly.

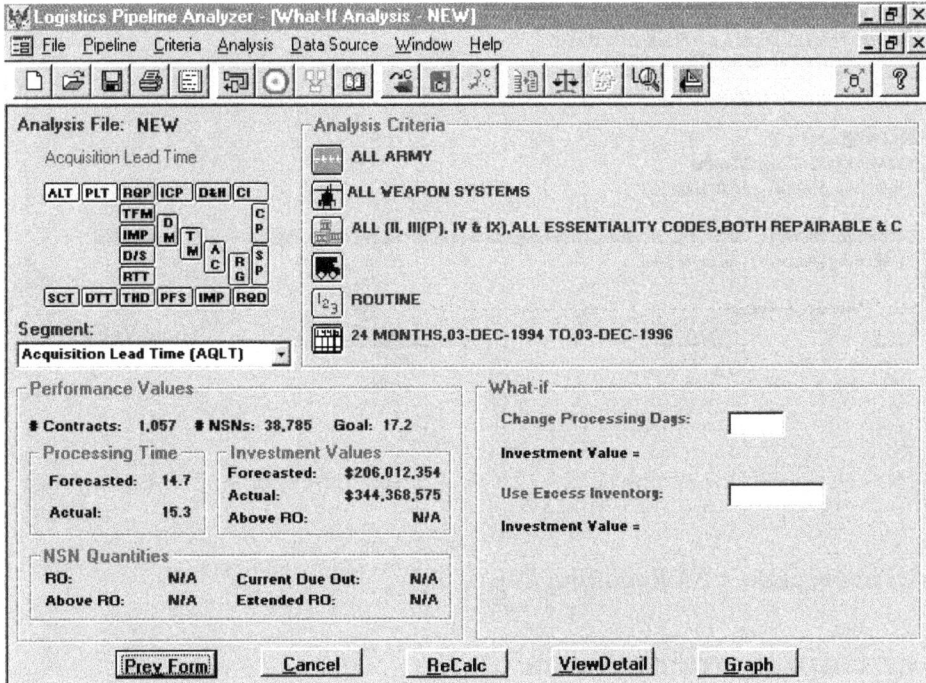

Figure 10.6 Example of the LPA What If Analysis Capability

Results Presentation

Another important feature of the LPA is its reporting capability. Reports and graphs can be generated by the LPA for any of the above analyses in both digital file and "hard copy" forms. Figure 10.7 shows an example of the LPA reporting capability. This provides the user with the ability to present findings to those at higher and lower levels of the organization to highlight opportunity areas and present justifications for the findings of the analysis. At a lower level of the organization, the user may provide the results of an analysis and ask subordinate managers for suggestions for improvements or rationale for current performance. At higher levels of the organization, the results from the LPA may be used to suggest and justify areas that by making policy or operating changes could improve the bottom line performance of the pipeline or pipeline segment. The presentation of the data and findings from analyses generated by the LPA can be used to increase understanding of the pipeline operations as a whole and initiate changes that optimize the time, resources, and dollar investment associated with logistics. Also, it can be used to determine the future impact based on policy change today.

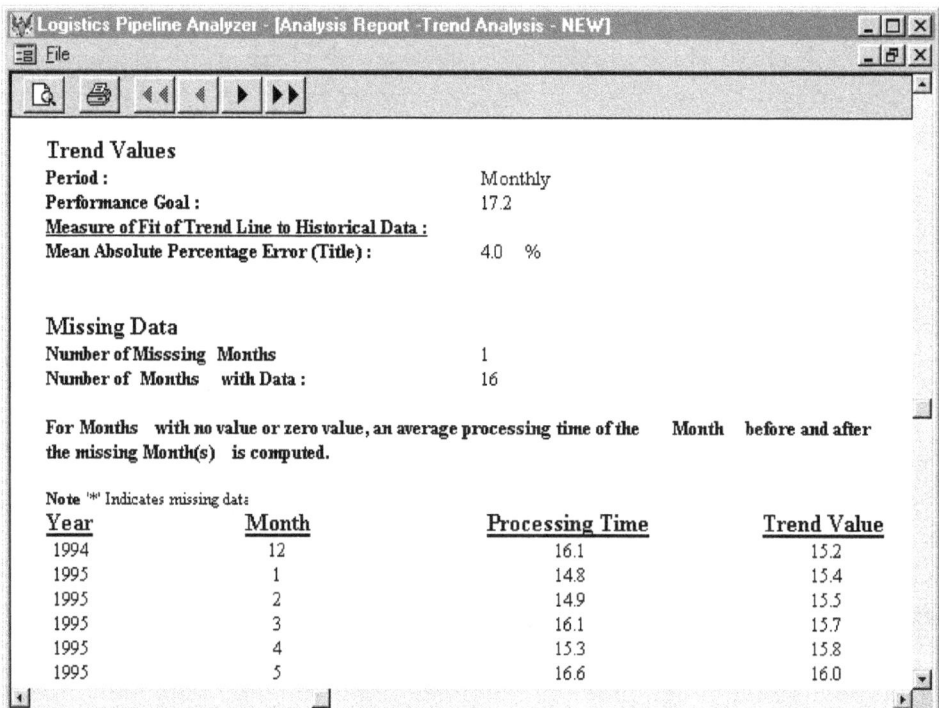

Logistics Pipeline Analyzer - [Analysis Report -Trend Analysis - NEW]

File

Trend Values
Period :   Monthly
Performance Goal :   17.2
Measure of Fit of Trend Line to Historical Data :
Mean Absolute Percentage Error (Title) :   4.0   %

Missing Data
Number of Missing Months   1
Number of Months   with Data :   16

For Months   with no value or zero value, an average processing time of the   Month   before and after the missing Month(s)   is computed.

Note '*' Indicates missing data

Year	Month	Processing Time	Trend Value
1994	12	16.1	15.2
1995	1	14.8	15.4
1995	2	14.9	15.5
1995	3	16.1	15.7
1995	4	15.3	15.8
1995	5	16.6	16.0

Figure 10.7 Example of the LPA Reporting Capability

10.5   Key Improvement Areas

The following concepts are fundamental in the improvement of operations of the future logistic system and the assurance of better pipeline management. They are applicable to any number of data systems for a variety of applications, both for the military and commercial applications.

- *Improved requirements determination.* The better we can forecast true demand and have confidence in the system that materiel or products will arrive when needed, the more we can reduce the safety stock in the system. This involves the quantification of better forecasts.

- *Streamlined business processes.* This required us to reduce the duplication of activities, and reduce the number of levels, people, and redundant stock. At the same time, we had to be more responsive with the ordering and the delivering of materiels, products, and supplies to the user.

- *Integrated customer and supplier requirements.* As the pipeline is defined and measured, performance goals are established. Successful performance is based not only on cost, but also on the quality of the service provided. Partnerships and trust must be a significant component of the customer and supplier relationship.

- *Tailored support.* A new strategy might incorporate an integrated combat capability and the quantity of weapon systems available and working, or the parts required for assembly in the commercial field. The pipeline must be flexible enough to meet differing requirements. Meeting war surge requirements or jumps in product demand is an integral part in the development of the pipeline management strategy.

- *Customer satisfaction.* Logistics services need to be tied to individual customer characteristics and customer requirements. The various classes of support can then be assigned associated fees. The pipeline must be designed so it can react to multiple dynamic scenarios, based on a changing business environment and changing business requirements.

- *Integrated logistics support continuum.* The repair and reutilization processes needed to be optimized to reduce materiel and costs. The repair cycle had to be directly incorporated into the pipeline strategy and new technology incorporated into the process to enhance repairables management.

- *Reduce inventory throughout the system.* When materiel, parts, assemblies, etc., needed to be stockpiled, we reduced the stock by giving better stock visibility through such concepts as total asset visibility (TAV) and by having better requirements determination. This reduced the safety stock required. This concept allowed the customer or users to view where all of the parts, etc., were located in the production or distribution facilities.

- *Faster assimilation of orders and faster delivery of materiel and parts.* The quicker materiel and parts orders can be processed and materiel and parts are delivered, the more inventory can be reduced in the system. The current implementation of objective supply capability (OSC) is improving this phase of the process.

- *Optimal parts mix.* This involves the identification of parts and their quantity to purchase a combination that best utilizes the limited budgets available and still achieves the highest possible production throughput or sustainability of forces and the required weapon systems. This required prioritization of parts so the most critical were identified and availability was ensured. We then determined the optimal mix of parts possible within the supply and budget constraints that maximized the production of key products and the readiness and sustainability of critical weapon systems.

The above example was a system developed for the military, but it has equal applicability of purchasing and tracking parts and assemblies in commercial production plant environments.

Chapter 11   Examples of Other Applications

11.1   Introduction

The examples in this chapter show how the process can be applied to a variety of companies and government agencies. Each of the examples described have different problems and products. The organizational goals, decision criteria, and metrics are also different, reflecting the individual needs of the organization, but the overall process is the same.

11.2   Product Life Cycle Management

Determining which products should be produced and which ideas should be developed for new products to develop is key to an organization's success. This involves developing a market strategy for research and development, managing product lines, and determining which products should be produced and which products should be dropped. Utilizing a structured process in making these decisions will provide a company with a framework for making product life cycle decisions and allocating resources to the most beneficial products for a company. The following two examples describe a structured methodology that can be used in the product life cycle determination. These are the same concepts that were introduced in the previous chapters.

11.3   Marketing Research Resource Allocation System

A decision support system was developed for a retail marketing corporation that prioritized marketing research programs and allocated resources to these programs. This system, along with its inherent decision making process, restructured the prioritization process across the organization. Both monetary and human resources were included in the prioritization and allocation process.

In most corporations, key individuals fund the marketing research projects they are interested in. Usually it is difficult to compare the merits of such diverse programs because the sets of decision criteria are not articulated well and agreed upon beforehand. To remedy this problem, a marketing research resource allocation system was developed based upon balancing the overall company objectives with the short- and long-term goals. The following set of objectives and decision criteria were used to evaluate the marketing research projects for one major corporation.

Retail Performance (Flagship Product Sales)

- What will be incremental sales the first year the proposed program is distributed nationally?

Retailer Focus (Retailer Sales)

- What will be the percent of total store retail sales growth for the retailer the first year the program is distributed nationally?

Industry Leadership

- Does this lead and grow the industry as a whole?
- Does this lead and grow the industry through innovation and product ideas and concepts?
- Does this strengthen our relationship with major customers?

Simplify the Business (Improve Productivity)

- Will this simplify business processes?
- Will this shorten times from idea to market?

Client Priority

- Rank projects based on clients' preferences.

Value Added by Research

- Breadth of support (who benefits?): This represents the extent to which the project benefits more than a single organizational unit. It is the applicability of research to other divisions.
- Will this minimize the risk for the programs to achieve success?
- Can other sources also be used for the information on determining the success of the program?
- How much will this contribute to achieving the objectives of the proposed program?

The system was developed and gave the user the ability to weight the decision criteria, prioritize projects with these criteria, and determine the sensitivity of the criteria used to make decisions. The system was constructed with a ranking model and operated in a user-friendly manner to be easily upgradeable, for users to be able to react instantaneously to changes in decision criteria over time, and to incorporate changes in the business climate.

11.5   Line Item Retention and Deletion

With the proliferation of products in the food industry and other business ventures, management must decide which of these items should be retained or deleted to allow for the introduction of new items. The approach in this decision process was to develop a ranking system that was dynamic and that considered a wide range of conflicting criteria in prioritizing which line items were to be deleted or retained from the product mix for a large food company. This provided corporate management with the ability to delete line items that were making the least contribution to overall corporate goals in a timely manner. These criteria included the following.

FINANCIAL CRITERIA
- Sales volume
- Dollar profitability
- Contribution to profit margin
- Obsolescence costs

MARKETING CRITERIA
- Future potential sales
- Competitive position
- Replacement potential
- Product line position
- Strategic importance

OPERATIONS CRITERIA
- Impact on overall quality
- Impact on sales
- Impact on operating costs
- Impact on production capacity

TECHNOLOGY CRITERION
- Impact on equipment

We were able to evaluate current and proposed products, weight the decision criteria, rank the product list, and do sensitivity and what if analyses to determine the overall best strategy for deletion and retention. The decision makers could quickly change the importance of the objectives and determine the new best strategy. This approach also provided management with the ability to continuously evaluate the line items on an ongoing basis and avoid wasting valuable resources.

Regional differences and preferences were also included in the deletion/retention decisions, and the cross regional impact was also evaluated. This capability had far reaching implications in helping management determine new product introduction. The system also can be used to determine the priority of products, and in determining the best production schedule and improved customer satisfaction. This information is important in other areas, such as product scheduling, planning, and life cycle evaluations.

11.5 Manpower Skill Mix Planning and Resource Allocation

A manpower planning decision model was developed for a telecommunications company to determine which projects were of greatest importance to accomplishing the business goals of the organization. It helped determine the appropriate skill mix of individuals required to complete these projects. Primary steps in the development process were developing criteria to evaluate the projects being worked on by the organization, defining the skill categories and skill levels needed for each project, defining the work units within the system, and formulating the decision model into an easy-to-use system that could adapt to their quickly changing environment.

Within the organization, fifty-six skills were identified that were required for the work, and five levels of skills could be utilized. With the system, these skills were reduced to several broad categories such as engineer, management, programmer, or specialist. This simplified the modeling and data requirements.

The work units were staff months, and they were defined in terms of resources and skills required for completing each of the projects. A skill level assignment also was made for any special skills required for a project. Resources and timing were also a part of the requirements to be satisfied before a project was undertaken.

The model included the ability to assign personnel to projects for personnel resource allocation, as well as manpower planning. The skills required for a project were matched to the project requirements, and resources were allocated based on timing, availability of resources, and the skills required and available for the task.

Criteria used to evaluate the projects were defined, the metrics and evaluation parameters (subjective scales or objective numbers) decided upon, and the data input structure was developed. Pertinent decision criteria were developed based on management discussions. A prioritization capability was incorporated into the model. The criteria used for the prioritization included:

- Return on equity impact
- Profit growth contribution
- Market share impact
- Customer satisfaction
- Employee satisfaction
- Operations cost reduction
- Infrastructure impact
- Time to first revenue

The prototype also provided decision makers with the ability to weight the decision criteria in the ranking. Criteria weighting included direct (normalized) weighting and pairwise comparison weighting capabilities.

To run the model, individuals were assigned to projects based on a general technical skill type, which included manager, engineer, programmer, or specialist. Each of these types also had several skill levels. Individuals were then assigned to the project by skill type and skill level. The number of staff months that the individual had available was matched with what was required to perform the project.

A staff month budget allocation was made for each project that included the minimum level of staff hours required for the project and the total hours required for the project. The project could not be performed if the minimum available hours were not enough to do the project.

Projects were then evaluated against the criteria. A ranking was performed. A resource allocation was performed in terms of staff hours, including value-based budgeting. Decisions were made about which projects would be completed or not completed by the company. This then drove the skill type and number of personnel that would be required for the completion of this work within a time limit.

This model incorporated two facets of corporate decision making: the types of projects that the organization undertook to support the long term objectives of the organization, and the types of individuals were required to develop the projects. The corporation could then look at the types of individuals that were available by skill type and skill level to decide whether additional or fewer individuals would be required to complete the workload. This process focused on the types of individuals required to meet their project base workload, while accomplishing the goals of the organization.

11.6   Summary

The central theme of this book is to employ methods that will enable the goals and objectives of an organization to become an integral part of the decision making process at all levels of the organization. This chapter, along with the overall modeling process and examples described in the book, show how this can be accomplished on a very practical level. Individuals within an organization that are key in structuring and making organizational decisions, should look closely at the concepts, examples, and applications, and hopefully utilize this process to develop a road map for the future of their company by making the best decisions possible.

The following is a list of e-book titles by the authors that provide additional examples of the applications of decision science methods. They may be of interest to the reader.

- *Developing a Warehouse and Inventory Level Optimization System*
- *Investment Strategy for Product Development in the Aerospace Industry*
- *Manpower Requirements for Management and Professional Personnel*
- *Strategic Planning and New Product Development*

Appendix A: An Overview of *A Professional's Guide to Decision Science and Problem Solving*

A.1   Introduction

Here we present an overview of the steps developed in our first book, *A Professional's Guide to Decision Science and Problem Solving*. A clear understanding of organizational objectives and goals provides direction and focus for the corporation. Typically, there are many different areas of opportunity to pursue for improvement with limited resources. A clear picture and evaluation of the organization's environment and the interaction between functions provides a framework for understanding and evaluating the issues facing the corporation. Sound assessment of the issues within the company is critical to pinpointing the areas for improving. Identifying and measuring these key areas provides an understanding of potential success in improvement. We feel the material in this book is a first step in any model and should be reviewed to ensure that the right goals and objectives are used.

One process is presented in the book that walks through the steps to identify corporate issues and develop solutions that can help the corporation improve. The structured thought process and solid evaluation of corporate functions and issues can help a corporation achieve improvement as measured by key performance metrics. This process provides a roadmap for identifying areas in which improvements can best be had. The later sections of the book explain this process, and case studies are presented applying the process to supply chain management, decision making surrounding new product development decisions, and key areas that should be assessed and analyzed in a corporate merger. The goal is for you to apply these concepts to your own organization.

Here is a summary and review of the chapters in *Professional Guide to Decision Science and Problem Solving*; this current book is a necessary extension of it. Figure A.1 shows an overview of the approach discussed in the book.

Overview of the Approach

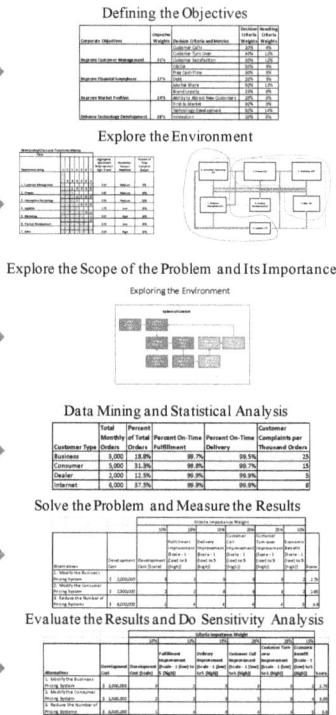

Steps in the Approach

Chapter 1: Define Corporate Objectives and Determine their Importance to Drive Organization Goals into Decisions

Chapter 2: Assess Functional Relationships, Benchmarks and Variability to Identify Integrated Corporate Opportunity Areas

Chapter 3: Perform High Level Business Process Modeling to Identify Cross-Functional Impacts

Chapter 4: Analyze Data to Understand Operational Performance

Chapter 5: Identify Cross-Functional Solutions

Chapter 6: Analyze the Sensitivity of Decisions to Arrive at the Best Results

Defining the Objectives

Explore the Environment

Explore the Scope of the Problem and Its Importance

Data Mining and Statistical Analysis

Solve the Problem and Measure the Results

Evaluate the Results and Do Sensitivity Analysis

Management Levels Required to Execute the Approach

Senior Executives Identify Problems, Establish Objectives and Establish Task Force with Executive Cross-Functional Representatives

Executive Cross-Functional Team Establishes Cross-Functional Project Team and Assesses Functional Relationships, Metrics, Performance and Cross-Functional Opportunity Areas

Project Team Models High Level Business Processes, Upstream and Downstream Impacts and Metrics for Opportunity Areas

Project Team Analyzes Original Source Operational Data to Quantify Performance and Identify Improvement Opportunities

Project Team Develops Potential Improvement Opportunities and Assesses their Viability Across the Impacted Functional Areas.

Project Team Performs Sensitivity and What-if Analysis and Presents Findings to Senior Executives

Figure A.1 Overview of the Approach

- Chapter 1, "Define the Objectives and Identify Metrics": You need to clearly articulate and document the objectives of a corporation. Each of the multiple functions within a company has different objectives with varying importance, and many of the high-level objectives of the corporation may conflict. It is vital for senior management to articulate these objectives and reach an overall consensus of the weighted importance so these objectives can be included in the corporate decision process at all levels.

- Chapter 2, "Explore the Environment": This chapter presents a new approach to integrated corporate planning. Assessments are made with key corporate functions to determine the closeness or dependence of the functional relationships you can use as a guide to identify the scope of the problem and which functional areas are included in the analysis. Additionally, benchmarking, variability analysis, and budget contributions are assessed to evaluate how well these functions perform against industry competitors.

- Chapter 3, "Explore the Scope of the Problem and Its Importance": It is critical in this analysis to not only identify the corporate issues, but also to determine their impact on the upstream and downstream processes, and the operational impact associated with improving these processes. High-level business process modeling is discussed. Often, fixing one problem can cause a problem in another area, and this step ensures that you address the operational impacts in the analysis.

- Chapter 4, "Data Mining and Statistical Analysis": This chapter highlights the importance of data analysis. Recognizing the problems and determining where improvements should be made is critical. Understanding the information that can quantify and support improvements provides a factual basis for justifying changes to operations and processes. This chapter presents a number of methods to analyze data with further detail of the methods provided in the appendices. (These methods are the focus of the current book.)

- Chapter 5, "Solve the Problem and Measure the Results": After the analysis is performed, which was shown in chapters 1 through 4, the approach to solving the problem is developed. Often, assessing the environment and performing the data analysis can lead to a clear solution or an approach. In other cases, you might require computer-based solutions or more sophisticated methods. The best solution is one that the decision maker understands and uses. This chapter focuses on determining the best methods that the data and environment can support and that the decision maker will use.

- Chapter 6, "Evaluate the Results and Do Sensitivity Analysis": This chapter discusses how to use the decision model to explore the results and determine their economic viability. A well-defined model has the functional capability to change key parameters and constraints and determine the impact of those changes on the final solution. What if analysis is a key ingredient in the decision process. The sensitivity of the variables in the solution must be tested to ensure that the best stable solution is reached.

- Chapter 7, "Summary of Part I": This chapter brings together the approach and highlights the key points from the analyses.

- Chapter 8, "Logistics Services Provider": This chapter applies the process to a full-service supply chain provider. The step-by-step analysis is performed to show how to implement this approach in the logistics environment.

- Chapter 9, "Life Cycle and New Product Development": This chapter applies the process to a company with its core competencies, and explains how new products can be developed. A structured approach to decision making is developed based on the interrelationships and performance of the company.

- Chapter 10, "Airline Merger": This chapter addresses some of the key considerations that need to be analyzed and assessed when two companies merge. Performance and functional interactions of the companies are assessed in order to ensure a successful merger. This is key to evaluating the activities for the airlines.

- Appendix A, "Overview of Decision Methodologies": This appendix provides a high level overview of various analytical and decision science methodologies that can be used to evaluate and formulate problem solutions. Again, this material is expanded in the current book.

- Appendix B, "Detailed Methodologies": This appendix provides the mathematical background for methods that are useful in model development. (Again, an extended treatment of these methods is the focus of the current book.)

Appendix B: Overview of Economic Analysis

B.1   Introduction

Understanding how to evaluate a number of alternatives from an economic perspective is important when making decisions in a company. As important as understanding the formulation of this evaluation is ensuring that all of the costs throughout the life cycle are captured and included in the decision making concept. This appendix provides an overview of these economic concepts.

B.2   Key Economic Analysis Principles

Interest and economic equivalence

"Interest" refers to the rental paid for the use of money. Normally, interest is quoted as a percent per year. Borrowers and lenders agree on an interest rate for a particular loan (either fixed or variable). The "going rate" is known as the market rate. Sometimes, the interest rate is called the "discount rate," the use is derived from certain investment instruments where the investor pays less than the face value and after the agreed term receives the face value, so the investor buys at simple and compound interest.

Simple interest is paid on the principal. Simple interest is very rare in practice. The main value of introducing simple interest is to start with the simplest conceptual form of interest, a discount.

$$I = Pni$$
where I = interest earned
P = principal amount
n = interest period in years
i = interest rate in % per year

Compounding Frequency

Compounding frequency refers to the frequency at which interest compounds. Interest is paid on both the principal and interest when interest is allowed to accrue.

$F = P(1+i)^n$

where F = Future or final value (principal + interest earned)

  P = principal amount

  n = number of compounding intervals

  i = interest rate in % per compounding interval

Compounding interest on a non-annual or annual basis for nominal and effective interest rates. Under more frequent compounding, the actual or effective interest rate is higher than the nominal interest rate.

$r = ci$

$i = \dfrac{r}{c}$

where r = nominal interest rate per year

  c = number of compounding intervals per year

  i = effective interest rate per compounding interval

Economic equivalence

If we compare two or more situations, their measures must be placed on an equivalent basis. Three key factors are involved in money equivalence: the amounts of the sums, the time of occurrence of the sums, and the interest rate. If I invest $x today, I would earn interest over time. At the end of the investment term, the amount of money held would be the principal plus interest. When we compare money amounts at different times, the interest effect needs to be considered. For investments over different time periods, replicate the investments to find a common denominator so that the investments have an equal life and then find the present value discounted cash flow. Annual equivalents can also be used to compare the two investments without replicating.

Money/Cash Flow Diagrams

Cash flow diagrams show the amounts and direction of cash flow events on a time line. This shows income or expense and when each occurs.

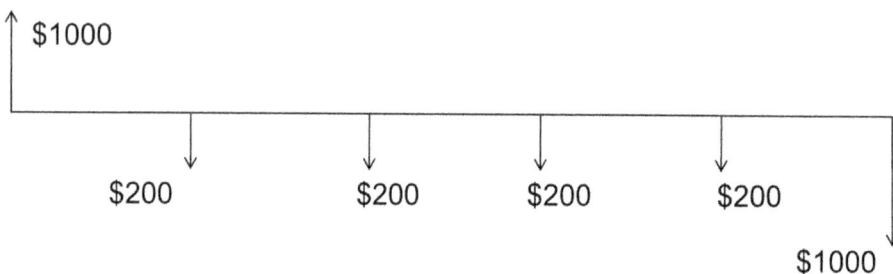

Interest Formula Basics

Let i = annual rate of interest

  P = amount at a time assumed to be the present

  n = number of compounding intervals

  A = single amount in a series of n equal amounts

   at the end of each period

  F = amount n interst periods hence

Single payment compound amount formula

This formula is useful where the loan is established and no payments are made before maturity, when the amount F must be paid. Interest factor tables based on the equivalence being sought, the interest rate, and n can be used to look up the value in the related interest rate table, or these formulas can be written in Excel.

$$F = P(1+i)^n$$

This can be inverted to yield the present value associated with some future amount. This formula is very useful for shifting future amounts to the present value.

$$P = F \frac{1}{(1+i)^n}$$

Equal payment series sinking fund formula

This situation occurs when one aims to set aside funds to pay off a future debt.

$$A = F \left[\frac{i}{(1+i)^n - 1} \right]$$

Equal payment series capital recovery formula

This situation occurs when one aims to recover an investment through a series of equal payments.

$$A = P \left[\frac{i(1+i)^n}{(1+i)^n - 1} \right] \Leftrightarrow P = A \left[\frac{(1+i)^n - 1}{i(1+i)^n} \right]$$

Equal payment series capital recovery formula

We know

  $A = F\,i/\,[(1+i)^n - 1]$

$$F = P (1 + i)^n.$$

Hence,

$$A = P\{[i (1 + i)^n]/[(1+i)^n - 1]\}$$

This is a formula to determine the value of a series of end-of-period payments, A, when the present sum, P, is known and is called the *uniform series capital recovery factor.*

Uniform gradient series formula

The money flows are divided into $n - 1$ distinct series with equal annual flows of G. The regular payments, A, vary according to a fixed gradient added to A_1.

$$A = A_1 + A_2$$

$$A_2 = G\left[\frac{1}{i} - \frac{n}{(1+i)^n - 1}\right]$$

where A_1 = flow at the end of the first year

G = annual change or gradient

n = number of years

A = annual equivalent equal amount

Comparison of proposals

The purpose of engineering economics is to enable a rational comparison of proposals. One possible measure is the present value, PV, of two proposals. PV compares the absolute dollar value of the comparison, but it does not compare this to the magnitude of the investment. Internal rate of return, IRR, provides a measure of the outcome normalized for magnitude.

Internal Rate of Return

The internal rate of return (IRR) is defined as the rate, i^*, which satisfies the equation:

$$0 = PV(i^*) = \sum_{t=0}^{n} \frac{F_t}{(1+i^*)^{-t}}$$

Organizations set their own threshold value of i^* to determine if a project is sufficiently "profitable." A value of i^* of approximately 30 percent is not unusual. IRR provides a meaningful measure of any project. The Present Equivalence (PE), Future Equivalence (FE) and Annual Equivalence (AE) can be used for the analysis. There may be several solutions to the equation when set to zero. Select the one that is reasonable and makes senses.

Method

- Define receipts and disbursements in regards to their time value of money.
- Set equal to zero.

- Solve for the interest rate that makes the receipts and disbursements equal (i.e., interest tables).
- Interpolate, if necessary, to determine the interest rate.

Payback period

Projects involve initial and sustainment costs. A common question is "How long until the cost of the project is recovered?" The payback period is the minimum value of n^* that satisfies:

$$0 \le \sum_{t=0}^{n^*} \frac{F_t}{(1+i)^{-t}}$$

Payback period is very useful in projects with a finite useful life.

In calculating the payback period, the revenue may be either actual cash received from sales of a product, or savings achieved as a result of the project. To compute, solve for the minimum n that satisfies the payback expression

Other formulations, such as the geometric-gradient series formula, are not addressed because of their infrequent use. Additionally, continuous compounding, used in theory sometimes, is not readily used in actuality and will not be covered in this book.

It should also be noted, that when you are evaluating projects with unequal life, you must find a multiple that results in a common lifetime.

B.3   Cost Breakdown Structure

The cost of activities within an organization must be assessed to understand their economic impact on processes, operations, and investments. Costs may be fixed, variable, reoccurring, or have one-time investment costs. Additionally, costs associated with ongoing maintenance, operations, repair, and disposal must also be included when analyzing problem areas. From a holistic perspective, life cycle costs from inception to disposal must be included. Project management and life cycle costing methodologies work to capture the entire set of related costs associated with an activity. These costs extend to marketing, training, disposal, overhead, and others that are not normally accounted for in the evaluation process.

A tool called a cost breakdown structure can be used to ensure that all of the associated costs with a project or activity are captured. This hierarchical diagram identifies typical costs that are found in a variety of different types of improvement activities or projects. There are four major categories of costs: research and development, investment, operations and maintenance, and system phase-out and disposal (Fabrycky and Blanchard, 1992). Project costs should be captured by category and year to account for each type of cost. Shown below is a corporate level diagram of a cost breakdown structure.

Cost Breakdown Structure

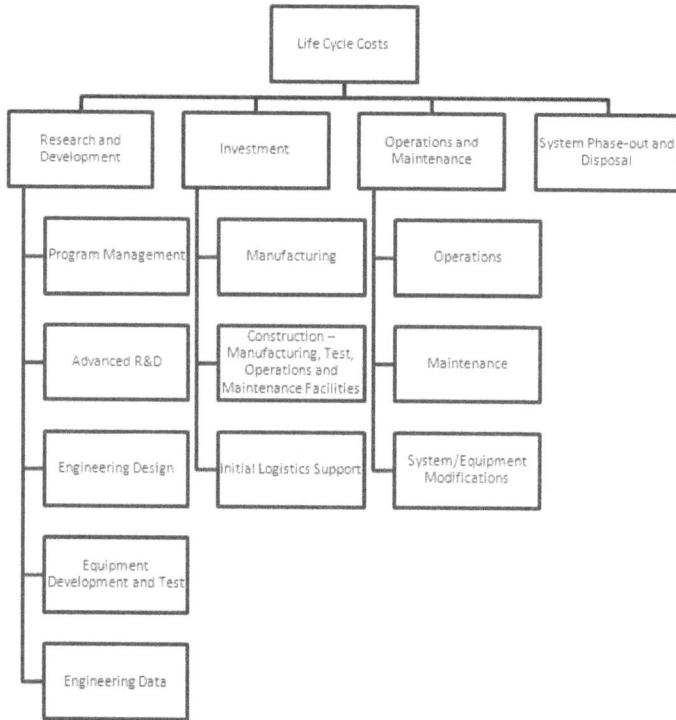

Figure B-1. Cost Breakdown Structure

Costs are incurred at a point in time and at a specified interest rate. Revenues/and or cost savings are also generated at a point in time. These cash flows or series of inflows and outflows of cash over time can be used to measure the profitability of a given activity. The time value of money and economic equivalence can be used to measure the inflows and outflows of cash and provide a point of comparison for these measures. Typically, the net present value, rate of return, or payback period is used to measure the profitability of the project. Numerous books and texts address these important concepts for the analysis of use of corporate resources. These economic considerations must be accounted for when determining various courses of action taken by a company.

B.4   Discounted Cash Flow Example

Table B.1 shows the general computations required to generate a discounted cash flow (DCF) business valuation. The approach to DCF business valuation described here is very simplistic. An experienced business valuator would provide additional insight, information, and technical knowledge in a real business valuation scenario. This may include assessing the quality of the management, the facilities, the efficiency of production, the current and future value of the product lines, and future growth potential. One would also assess competition and if there are any barriers that protect the company, e.g., patents or proprietary technology. If it is a new product, the initial costs to put it into business should be assessed, as well as whether or not it has synergies with current operations.

In this example, there is a detailed four-year forecast for the years 2001 through 2004. After this point, the continuing value of the firm is computed. We are assuming that the predictions for the performance metrics would have been made in the year 2000 and that the data used in this example for Company A would be predictions for the years 2001–2004.

Table B.1. Computations for Generating Discounted Cash Flow

Prediction Year for Company A	Company A 2001	Company A 2002	Company A 2003	Company A 2004
Predicted Net Operating Profit by Year (in millions)	$29	$60	$65	$77
Estimated Amortization	$2	$5	$3	$2
Operating Earnings before Interest, Taxes, and Amortization (EBITA)	$31	$65	$68	$79
Taxes on EBITA (39%)	$12	$25	$27	$31
Changes in Deferred Taxes	-$8	-$9	-$6	-$11
Net Operating Profit Less Accumulated Taxes (NOPLAT)	**$11**	**$31**	**$35**	**$37**
Net Investment	-$9	-$11	-$5	-$5
Free Cash Flow	**$2**	**$20**	**$30**	**$32**
Weighted Average Cost of Capital (WACC)	6.7%	6.7%	6.7%	6.7%
Present Value of Cash Flows	$2	$17	$24	$23
Total Present Value of Cash Flows in 5-Year Planning Horizon	**$66**			
Return on Invested Capital (ROIC) in Perpetuity	15%			
Expected Growth Rate in NOPLAT in Perpetuity (g)	5%			
Weighted Average Cost of Capital (WACC) in Perpetuity	6.7%			
Continuing Value	**$1,458**			
Present Value of Free Cash Flow Years 1–4	$66			
Present Value of Continuing Value (discounted at WACC in perpetuity)	$1,055			
Operating Value	**$1,120**			
Equity Value (Operating Value + Market Value of Nonoperating Assets – Debt and Nonequity Sources of Financing) *Example for this case*	$1,123			
Most Recent Shares Outstanding (in millions)	50			
Price Per Share	$22.46			

Each of the terms used in the table above are briefly described below.

1. Predicted Net Operating Profit by Year (in millions): This is a prediction of the Net Operating Profit by year.
2. Estimated Amortization: Amortization is included in the NOP projection, so it must be removed from the prediction. Estimates are made regarding these quantities.
3. Operating Earnings before Interest, Taxes, and Amortization (EBITA): This is the operating earnings before interest, taxes, and amortization with amortization.
4. Taxes on EBITA (39%): Taxes on EBITA were determined by using an estimated tax rate of 39% applied to EBITA.
5. Changes in Deferred Taxes: Changes to the deferred taxes referred to actual income taxes adjusted to a cash basis. For this example, they were estimated and used in this forecast.
6. Net Operating Profit Less Accumulated Taxes (NOPLAT): This represents the after-tax operating profits of the company after adjusting the taxes to a cash basis.
7. Net Investment: Net investment is the change in invested capital. Invested capital is the capital invested in the company by shareholders and creditors and operating and other non-operating activities.
8. Free Cash Flow (FCF): Free cash flow is a company's true operating cash flow. It is the total after-tax cash flow generated by the company to all providers of the company's capital.
9. Weighted Average Cost of Capital (WACC): The opportunity costs to all the capital providers weighted by their relative contribution to the company's total capital.
10. Present Value of Cash Flows: This is the free cash flow discounted to the present value using the WACC as the discount rate.
11. Total Present Value of Cash Flows in 4-Year Planning Horizon: Sum of cash flows for five-year planning horizon.
12. Return on Invested Capital (ROIC) in Perpetuity: The return on invested capital is the NOPLAT divided by the invested capital. In this case, it is an estimate of the ROIC projected for the years used to determine the continuing value of a company.
13. Expected Growth Rate in NOPLAT in Perpetuity (g): This is the expected growth rate in NOPLAT for the years used to determine the continuing value of a company.
14. Weighted Average Cost of Capital (WACC) in Perpetuity: This is the WACC for the years used to determine the continuing value of a company.
15. Continuing Value: This is the resulting computation for the continuing value of a company. The base for the continuing value is shown in the table above and is the average NOPLAT over the shorter-term planning horizon.
16. Present Value of Free Cash Flow Years 1–4: This is the free cash flow discounted over the forecast horizon. In this case, a five-year horizon was used.
17. Present Value of Continuing Value (discounted at WACC in perpetuity): This is the quantity computed for the continuing value of the company discounted back to the present value.

18. Operating Value: This is the sum of the present value of the FCF for years 1–4 and the present value of the continuing value of the firm.

19. Equity Value (Operating Value + Market Value of Non-operating Assets – Debt and Non-equity Sources of Financing): The equity value is the operating value of the firm plus the market value of non-operating assets minus the debt and non-equity sources of financing. The equity value of the firm can be used to estimate the share price of a stock. In this example, the operating value has been increased by $2.4 million to demonstrate this concept.

20. Most Recent Shares Outstanding: This is the most recent estimate of the shares outstanding for the company.

21. Price Per Share: The price per share is the equity value of the stock divided by the most recent outstanding shares.

The result of this example shows the operating value of the firm at $1,120 million and the resulting price per share of the firm at $22.46 per share. One of the primary inputs into the DCF calculation is the net operating profit, which is a predicted value. The other inputs into the DCF would be based on accounting information. This shows how the predicted net operating profit integrates with the business valuation process.

References

Cassone, Deandra T. Dissertation: "A Process to Estimate the Value of a Company Using Operational Performance Metrics," Kansas State University, 2005.

Hwang, Ching-Lai, and Masud, Abu Syed Md. *Multiple Objective Decision Making—Methods and Applications*, Springer-Verlag, Berlin, Germany, 1979.

Hwang, Ching-Lai, and Ming-Jen Lin. *Group Decision Making Under Multiple Criteria*, Springer-Verlag, Berlin, Germany, 1987.

Hwang, Ching-Lai, and K. Yoon. *Multiple Attribute Decision Making Methods and Applications*, A State-of-the-Art Survey," Springer-Verlag, Berlin, Germany, 1981.

Tillman, Frank A., Cassone, Deandra T., *A Professional's Guide to Decision Science and Problem Solving: An Integrated Approach for Assessing Issues, Finding Solutions, and Reaching Corporate Objectives*, Upper Saddle River, NJ, Financial Times Press/Pearson Education, Web: December 1, 2012, Hardcover: February 2012.

Tillman, Frank A., Cassone, Deandra T., *Developing a Warehouse and Inventory Level Optimization System*, Financial Times Press/Pearson Education, Upper Saddle River, NJ, Web. May 31, 2012.

Tillman, Frank A., Cassone, Deandra T., *Investment Strategy for Product Development in the Aerospace Industry*, Financial Times Press/Pearson Education, Upper Saddle River, NJ, Web. May 31, 2012.

Tillman, Frank A., Cassone, Deandra T., *Manpower Requirements for Management and Professional Personnel*, Financial Times Press/Pearson Education, Upper Saddle River, NJ, Web. May 18, 2012.

Tillman, Frank A., Cassone, Deandra T., *Strategic Planning and New Product Development*, Financial Times Press/Pearson Education, Upper Saddle River, NJ, Web. May 31, 2012.

Tillman, Frank A., Deandra T. Cassone, *Integrated Business Decisions, Analyses, and Strategies*, Textbook self-published for use in courses at Kansas State University, College of Business Administration, MBA Program, 2002.

Wolter J. Fabrycky, and Benjamin S. Blanchard. *Life-Cycle Cost and Economic Analysis*, Prentice Hall, 1991.

Yoon, K. Paul, and Ching-Lai Hwang. *Multiple Attribute Decision Making—An Introduction, Series: Quantitative Applications in the Social Sciences*, A Sage University Paper, 104, Thousand Oaks, CA: Sage, 1995.

Dedication

Frank A. Tillman, PhD, PE
July 22, 1937 – February 26, 2017

Frank was born July 22, 1937 in Linn, Missouri. The unfortunate early passing of his father started him working at the age of nine. This work ethic carried throughout his life. Frank was an athlete through high school and went to college at Lincoln University on a basketball scholarship. He soon realized that academia was his passion. Frank was married to Barbara Langendoerfer and they shared 58 years together at the time of his death. Working full-time to support his family and going to school full-time he earned a Bachelors and Master's Degree in Industrial Engineering from the University of Missouri. He worked at Standard Oil of Ohio and attended Case Institute working on his Ph.D. in Operations Research. He was awarded a Ford Foundation grant to finish his Ph.D. at the University of Iowa in Industrial Engineering.

After graduating, he moved his family to Manhattan, Kansas and took a position as a Professor at Kansas State University. A year later, at 29, he became Head of the Department of Industrial Engineering. Frank loved academics. He mentored many students throughout his career that have become very successful and kept in touch with him over time. As Professor and Department Head, he was instrumental in the approval of the engineering PhD program, he was a founder of the KSU Chapter of Tau Beta Pi, and was involved in Alpha Pi Mu, ABET accreditation, was an Institute of Industrial Engineering fellow, wrote fifty-four papers and two books during his time on the faculty and was awarded emeritus status upon his departure from the university. Frank was also inducted into the KSU Engineering Hall of Fame. Frank began his real estate development career during this time as well, developing a number of housing communities in Manhattan, Kansas. In 1972, he received a Presidential appointment to U.S. President Nixon's Price Commission and moved his family to Washington DC for a short time.

He began consulting businesses which drew him from academia to the business world as his primary career. He operated two successful consulting companies with many contracts with government agencies and Fortune 500 companies. He spent the next twenty years managing these firms with offices in Manhattan and Washington DC. Frank also continued his real estate activities with commercial and residential real estate. In Frank's later years, he published four books and four eBooks documenting his approach to problem solving and applying theory to practical solutions.

Frank was very active in the community. He served two terms on the USD 383 School Board, served on multiple advisory councils and coached numerous basketball, softball and baseball teams. His Youth Activities Foundation supported numerous sports teams in Manhattan and Kansas City. Frank and Barbara additionally support a scholarship fund for Industrial Engineering students and were Seaton Founders for the College of Engineering. One of his most treasured activities was coffee in the morning with KSU faculty and community members.

Of all of his abilities and passions, his family was always first and foremost to him. He was a man that cared for his family deeply and provided for them unceasingly. He was very involved in their lives and was happy to take them on family vacations to Disney World, ski trips, the Lake of the Ozarks and helping his kids and grandkids through college.

Frank touched many lives in his time here on earth, including students, athletes, business community members, faculty and friends. He always saw potential in people who were discouraged in engineering. He endlessly recruited for the Industrial Engineering Department. He always had an opinion and was happy to discuss it with you.

For me personally, he was my father, my mentor and my friend and he is deeply missed.

Deandra Cassone, PhD, PMP

www.ingramcontent.com/pod-product-compliance
Lightning Source LLC
Chambersburg PA
CBHW081508200326
41518CB00015B/2428